Superhints
for Gardeners

also compiled by the Lady Wardington

SUPERHINTS

SUPERHINTS FOR COOKS

Superhints
for Gardeners

FROM THE GREAT AND
GREEN-FINGERED

Compiled by
the Lady Wardington

MICHAEL JOSEPH

LONDON

MICHAEL JOSEPH LTD

Published by the Penguin Group
27 Wrights Lane, London W8 5TZ
Viking Penguin Inc., 375 Hudson Street, New York, New York
10014, USA
Penguin Books Australia Ltd, Ringwood, Victoria, Australia
Penguin Books Canada Ltd, 10 Alcorn Avenue, Toronto, Ontario,
Canada M4V 3B2
Penguin Books (NZ) Ltd, 182-190 Wairau Road,
Auckland 10, New Zealand

Penguin Books Ltd, Registered Offices: Harmondsworth,
Middlesex, England

First published in Great Britain 1993
Second impression October 1993
Third impression November 1993
Fourth impression December 1993
Fifth impression October 1994
Sixth impression October 1995

Typeset in Goudy 10/13 point
Printed in England by Butler & Tanner Ltd, Frome and London
Design and computer page make-up by Penny Mills

A CIP catalogue record for this book is available from
the British Library

ISBN 0 7181 3660 8

The moral right of the author has been asserted

The hints in this book are intended to suggest possible
solutions only. While every effort has been made to check
their accuracy, the compiler, contributors and publisher can
neither guarantee absolute success nor accept any legal
responsibility or liability for their effectiveness.

❖❖❖ Contents ❖❖❖

KATHARINE HOUSE HOSPICE

Life is terminal and all too often cancer is the terminator. At the Katharine House Hospice at Adderbury near Banbury, Oxfordshire, along with many other hospices up and down the country, the aim is to alleviate the misery and suffering endured by patients beset with this disease.

The desperate need for terminal care in our area was brought home to Neil Gadsby, the founder of the Hospice, when Katharine, his gifted only daughter, died slowly of cancer when she was twenty. Having lived through this experience he retired from being a schoolmaster and, with a group of like-minded people, set about founding a place where patients could receive treatment, and their families and carers could find comfort and encouragement.

To this end, alongside specialist nursing and medicine, many complementary therapies designed to give the highest possible quality of life for each individual have been introduced. Patients come to the Katharine House Hospice for pain control, special dressings and medical care, and sympathetic help in coming to terms with their situation.

In addition to a day unit, there are attractive sun-filled rooms where patients can stay for perhaps a week or two to adjust their treatment and give their families a much-needed rest from nursing their loved ones. Finally the Hospice provides a dignified and peaceful end to life if, for any reason, the appropriate care can't be given at home.

Although a loyal band of voluntary workers back up the professional nursing staff and the Macmillan nurses based there, this independent Hospice is always in need of funds. As I write, it costs £1,000 a day to keep the wheels turning and as you read, this figure will have almost certainly increased. Last days are very precious both to the dying and the bereaved and should be as peaceful and pain-free as it is humanly possible to make them. To my mind there is no more important cause to support, and that is why I am giving all the the royalties from this book to the Katharine House Hospice.

The Lady Wardington

NOTE

Horticulturists, designers, curators, writers, broad-casters and green-fingered enthusiasts along with owners of great gardens have generously donated ideas culled from years of 'hands-on' experience, and I am eternally grateful to them all for sharing their expertise and making this book possible. I just wish that space had permitted every hint to be included and can only apologize to the people whose ideas are not here.

Where addresses are given the gardens are open to be visited, either on their own account or for the National Gardens Scheme, in which case their opening dates and addresses can be found in the NGS Yellow Book. The gardens in Borsetshire will be familiar to Radio 4 listeners, who will know that they can only be visited in the imagination.

Audrey Waddington

PLANNING AND
MAINTENANCE

NEW BROOMS

When you buy a new house, be braced to spend 5 per cent of the value of the property on the garden. If you have builders in, make sure there is a clause in the contract ensuring that repairs of any damage done by them in the garden is at their expense but that the reparations can be done by another firm. Finding a good garden contractor in a new area can be tricky: write to BALI, the British Association of Landscape Industries, for a list of local people.

Nicholas Bell
Practicality Brown, garden contractor

PIGGY

A completely overgrown and derelict garden can be reclaimed by keeping free-range pigs. Use an electric fence to contain them and let them gradually work over the entire garden, one section at a time.

A. W. A. Baker
Old Rectory Cottage, Berks

11

PLAYING THE GOAT

If you inherit a large unmanageable garden buy a goat. These animals are extremely tidy-minded gardeners and as aromatic as any herb. While he is undertaking his job as head gardener (we did this in our moat) go out and visit other people's gardens and enjoy yourself.

Mrs C. H. A. Bott
Benington Lordship, Herts

GIDDY GOAT

Goats can play havoc with your garden. Ensure that your neighbours keep theirs safely secured.

Mr and Mrs Phillip Archer
Brookfield Farm, Borsetshire

BEGIN AT THE END

When starting to make a new garden always start at the point furthest from the house. By the time you have worked back you will have made most of your mistakes – and they won't stare you in the face as you sit outside your drawing-room windows having an evening drink.

H H Judge Patrick Medd
Little Place, Oxon

STARTING FROM SCRATCH

Always complete the moving of heavy material across the garden before preparing and laying the lawn. Then before sowing the lawnseed lay a strip of turf round the perimeter following the shape of the lawn so that a firm edge can be cut within a week or two. If you want to economize, cut each piece of turf lengthwise – it will go twice as far.

Geoffrey Coombs
Garden adviser

12

CULTIVATE THE CRACKS

If you find mowing a bore, you could either allow the lawn to become a piece of flowering meadow or else dispense with it altogether and pave it over, either as a sitting-out area or to colonize with plants that love to grow in paving cracks. Not all of these should be creeping or mat-forming like thymes or rock roses; let some be tall and graceful, like the wand flower, or stately, like mulleins.

Christopher Lloyd
Gardening correspondent, Country Life

SECOND THOUGHTS

Thinking of increasing the size of your garden? Don't. Consider the costs in five years' time, the extra labour involved and your diminishing energy.

Mrs John Montagu
Mapperton, Dorset

MIX AND MATCH

If you have a very small garden, why not grow vegetables and flowers together? Runner beans with sweet peas, lettuces with lobelia etc.

Kenneth Vaughan
Gardener-in-charge, Westbury Court Garden, Glos

VISUAL SPACE

To make a small garden appear larger, plant hot colours such as reds, oranges and yellows close to the house and cool blues, greys and mauves further away to give a sense of distance.

Stella Caws
Landscape and garden designer

DO IT WITH MIRRORS

Use mirrors to add surprise and intrigue as well as distance to the garden, but always site them at an angle to the main approach – nothing spoils the illusion more than one's own reflection.

Christina Oates
Secret Garden Designs

LOST IN THE WILDERNESS

If your garden is too big, accept the fact. Ours is, and 'beyond the laurel' is jungle, impassable, possibly the home of large animals. Guests, from whom we have not heard of late, may be lost there. We call it 'reservation' or 'wild place' or 'butterfly reserve', and are at peace.

David Kossoff
Actor and author

THE FINISHING TOUCH

The final touch to a garden can be a statue. Our garden pivots on Aphrodite, the Greek goddess of love. She adds a touch of elegance by day and a sense of magic by night. She is perfectly complemented by the Ambridge Rose. It flowers freely and continuously, has a neat bushy growth and the apricot-pink flowers are cupped at first and open into loose rosettes. You can get it from David Austin Roses.

Mr and Mrs Jack Woolley
The Lodge, Ambridge, Borsetshire

STONECROP

Almost anything will grow well in gravel and in difficult places such as under trees it can be invaluable. Lay it about 4 in/10 cm deep and it will act as a mulch. Why not have a gravel river flowing through the garden, with all manner of plants from rock roses to shrubs growing in it?

Valerie Aisher
Garden designer

FOLLOW YOUR NOSE

Trust your own instinct whatever the book says.

Patrick Braddell
*Treasurer, Simon Weatherby Garden Trust,
Katharine House Hospice*

EAST, WEST, HOME'S BEST

Always buy at a local nursery – they know what suits the area. Look at local gardens. Don't try to beat nature. Exotica might flourish in a very favoured situations, but not in wild or windy places or frost pockets – or where marauding rabbits or hungry sheep abound.

Katie Boyle
TV and radio personality

HOMESICK

Learning about the natural habitat of plants brought in from other parts of the world is a great help in ensuring that we provide them with growing conditions as close as possible to the ones they enjoy in their homelands.

Michael Garsten
Retired plantsman

ECONOMIZE

Buy small plants – they are much cheaper and less likely to be pot-bound – and transplant them into 9 in/23 cm pots until they are well rooted. Once they reach that stage there is less danger that they will be submerged by other plants when they are planted out.

Christopher Wells
Reynolds Farm, Berks

MONEY WELL SPENT

Spend 25 centimes on buying a plant but 150 centimes on planting it.

Princess Sturdza
Le Vastiveral, France

EMBARRAS DE RICHESSE

Gardening seems to consist of greed and indigestion. Greed because you can't resist buying a plant. Indigestion because there is no more room for it.

Christopher Wells
Reynolds Farm, Berks

PICK A POSY

Before you decide where to put a new plant, make a posy with its leaves and flowers and those of the plants to which it might be adjacent. In this way you will see whether it will look happy in their company when it is in the garden.

The Hon. Mrs Price
Pettifers, Oxon

RULE OF THREE

When attempting to place a difficult plant, try it in three positions in the garden. First, where you think it

16

will grow best. Second, where you wish it to grow. Third, the least suitable spot, where no one will see it. It is here that it will thrive.

Ian Kirby,
Dip. Hort.(Kew)

LOTS OF A GOOD THING

If a plant is good, have a lot of it – nothing is worse than a 'dotty' appearance. Generally think in areas of at least 1 sq. yd/0·83 sq. m. Drifts are more natural than circles of herbaceous plants as preached by Gertrude Jekyll.

Patricia Elkington
Garden designer

MORE THAN ONE

When choosing plants, I follow the principle that they should fulfil more than one of the following criteria:

1. give a display more than once in a year.
2. be useful as a cut flower.
3. provide a bewitching scent.
4. give weed-suppressing ground cover.

The Lord Feversham
Duncombe Park, N Yorks

MOON TIME

'Always plant on a waxing moon, never on a waning moon.' Apparently water in the ground, not just the seas, responds to the moon's cycles, so that it *is* better to plant when the water is rising.

The late Denholm Elliott
Actor

THE BIGGER THE HOLE

Whenever planting from a container make sure you dig a big enough hole. It must be at least twice the size of the pot and the base should be well forked up. Incorporate lots of good stuff such as old potting compost, peat and Blood, Fish and Bone, with the existing soil and water well before and after.

Brian Hutchinson
Head gardener, Castle Howard, N Yorks

PLANT WITH A POT

Sink a flowerpot full of gravel alongside a new plant whose roots are going to need plenty of water. When watering, water into the pot.

The late Monica Dickens
Author

BOTTOMS UP

'What are these inverted pots doing all over the garden?' I once asked 'Cherry' Ingram (Captain Collingwood Ingram), the celebrated collector and hybridizer of cherries and other trees and shrubs. 'Are they for sea-kale?' 'Of course not,' he said rather crossly, 'I have been moving plants around and the weather is dry; you can transplant at any time if you cover the plants with clay pots to keep the moisture in. You can leave them unwatered for as much as a week.' He picked up the pot and showed me the damp soil underneath. Cherry was 98 then and lived to be 101, gardening to the end.

Anne Scott-James
Journalist

SETTLING IN

If you want to move a plant at any time of the year, even when it is well grown and in full flower, dig a reasonably large hole and fill it with boiling water before putting in your leaf mould or compost mixture. If necessary use two or three kettlefuls. This takes the chill out of the ground and the plant or shrub should settle nicely.

The Duke of Buccleuch
Boughton House, Northants

ALWAYS APART

Contrary to popular belief, invasive plants, particularly those whose roots spread below the surface, can be kept apart and under control with strips of lawn-edging inserted into the soil.

Michael Garsten
Retired plantsman

CLARET COMPASS

A claret bottle filled with sand and attached by string to a stake makes a good compass for marking out circular designs such as knot gardens, potagers etc. Just dribble the sand out of the bottle, holding it taut at the end of the string as you make the circle.

The Lady Fanshawe

TURNING FULL CIRCLE

When we were redesigning the grounds here we made sure that, when planning shrubberies and enlarging flower-beds, the outlines conformed to the turning circles of the lawn-mower. This makes mowing simple and eliminates endless stops and starts.

Professor Gerald Benney
Beenham House, Berks

RING BINDERS

The rings from old barrels are excellent for marking bulb plantings or sowings of annuals in a border.

The Hon. Lady Butler

GO WITH THE FLOW

A curving edge to a flower border is usually more attractive than a straight one but difficult to plan and mark out. A hose pipe laid along the projected line will give a good idea of how it will look and can be adjusted to get it just right by a kick here and there. But you can't dig against the pipe without knocking it out of position, so mark its line by sprinkling sand along it, then dig along the sandy line.

Vernon Russell-Smith
Garden designer

... I use this method, never finalizing until I have viewed the line from every angle, including upstairs windows. And if there is no hurry to get on with the job, once the pipe has been left in place for a few days the grass underneath will have blanched, marking the cutting line.

Robert (Oz) Osborne
Head gardener, Martineau Environmental Studies Centre, Birmingham

KEEP OFF THE GRASS

Put a path between the lawn and the border to give the plants somewhere to flop without killing the lawn underneath. Or use a low hedge to contain borders in which soft billowing plants are grown. It will provide support and again, keep the plants from spilling on to the grass.

Christina Oates
Secret Garden Designs

MOWN OVER

An over-large, under-manned garden can become manageable and enjoyable if you eliminate all flower-beds, plant lots of shrubs and buy the biggest and best sit-on mower you can afford.

Christopher Courage
Edgecote House, Northants

MAKE A RECORD

If you have a mixed herbaceous border which also contains spring bulbs, take a photograph of the daffodils in April and of the tulips in May. You will then see where to plant and – more important, perhaps – where not, for fear of digging the bulbs up when winter comes.

Evelyn Anthony
Author

AIDE MEMOIRE

This is an aid to remind one where bulbs (and any other plants that die down completely) are located. I save raspberry canes and cut them into 5 in/12·7 cm lengths, then put two or three round the spot, sinking them into the ground so that only 1 in/2·5 cm is left showing. Very soon, they are almost invisible and only the gardener can spot them.

Mrs H. S. Hodding
Westcott House, Bucks

MAKE A NOTE

Always carry a biro and a small tear-off notebook in your gardening jacket pocket and *never* take them out. Any ideas you have or jobs you see that need to be done can then be written down immediately and dealt with later.

Mrs Peter Toynbee
NGS Hon. County Organizer, Bucks

REMEMBERING

I find it hard to remember just when to do what in my garden – pruning, particularly. Now I have bought a 'Gardener's Year' book and under the appropriate month make notes such as 'prune clematis under dining-room window' or – what often gets forgotten in June – 'sow wallflowers'.

Orlando Murrin
Deputy editor, Living

BURIED MEMOS

Here is a fail-safe way of dealing with plants that require pruning at different times of the year – clematis, for example. Write the pruning instructions on a piece of card and place it in a small, sealed plastic bag ½ in/1.25 cm under the soil at the base of the stem when planting out.

Mrs J.W. Law
Swerford Park, Oxon

WARM AND DRY

Some of the most desirable plants are slightly tender ones. Protecting them with straw, bracken, fine netting or mulching does not always work, especially in severe winters because of the dampness. A more successful method is to pile polystyrene granules around the plant, retained with fine plastic netting and canes. These keep the plant both warm and dry while still allowing air to get to it.

Myles Challis
1 Lister Road, London E11

CHILD LABOUR

If you want your children to help and be interested in the garden, make sure you pay them the going rate. This is what my father did to me. The fact that I sloped off quite soon didn't prevent it from being a rewarding experience.

Alexandra Heseltine

DIVINE INTERVENTION

God is the best gardener. Now that the Meteorological Office is so much better at divining the weather, follow the forecasts carefully. Save water bills by not watering when you know it will rain and always hoe when you know the sun will shine so the weeds shrivel immediately.

Sue Minter
Curator, Chelsea Physic Garden

THE ARTFUL DODGER

This advice is for the idle man who likes to enjoy his garden restfully. Encourage your wife to work in the garden. Point out the benefits to her health and peace of mind. Praise her efforts. Refrain from criticizing her failures. Use every artful trick to persuade her to work hard to create a garden for your enjoyment.

The Lord Prentice

TAKE A BREAK

A garden – remember to sit in it.

The Lady Saye and Sele
Broughton Castle, Oxon

SLUGGISH

Some garden work is better left undone. Remember that a human being does at least as much damage relatively as a slug!

Joan Loraine
Garden designer

BUSY DOING NOTHING

I have achieved a state of masterly inactivity in at least one part of my garden. I have an area roughly 25ft x 40ft/7·6m x 12·19m which is basically shrubbery with a few trees. It took a while to eliminate pernicious weeds such as twitch and bellweed but now, if I resist the urge to hoe, I not only get a succession of spring bulbs, but also, in season, primroses and foxgloves which are seeding and spreading. The leaves from the trees lie undisturbed, mulching and top-dressing the bulbs and flowers, while birds find something of interest either in the berries or grubbing about among the leaves. From the first snowdrop to the last berry, there is always something happening there.

Michael Hudson

TWO INTO ONE WILL GO

My small garden is 7 yd/6·5 m wide by 25 yd/23 m long. The intensive system of growing that has evolved in this small space calls for a high level of nutrition and it is necessary to feed regularly with a complete compound fertilizer. I add a proprietary foliar feed to the spray against aphids etc. using a spray gun attached to the garden hose, and get round using just 2 gal/9 l thus killing and feeding at the same time.

Mrs A. Dexter
23 Beechcroft Road, Oxford

FEED 'EM UP

Remember to feed your plants – they are like children, you cannot just feed them once and then forget about them.

Patricia Elkington
Garden designer

24

PICK-ME-UP

Epsom salts applied to sickly plants (2 oz/56 gr salts to 2 gal/9 l water) as a drench brings back the green more often than not.

Paul Miles
Garden designer

THE END PRODUCT

Get a donkey. All it will need is a shed and some space. Rescue one and keep it warm in winter and cool in summer. It likes a varied diet: weeds, cut thistles, rose clippings and all herbaceous perennials cut down after flowering. Add some grass in summer and hay in winter and what goes in one end comes out the other as excellent manure. Much cheaper and more companionable than a shredder.

Jill Cowley
Garden designer

CHIPS OFF THE BLOCK

Chippings produced from tree pruning or stump grinding can provide a cheap and useful mulch, but they do tend to starve the plants they surround by removing nitrogen from the soil. Avoid this problem by adding fertilizer containing nitrogen to the mulch. N. B. Do not dig wood chippings into the soil.

Ian Cooke
Head gardener, Ascott, Bucks

HEALTHY HEATHERS

Grass cuttings are best used as a mulch around ericaceous plants, as they release a tremendous amount of nitrogen when they break down, raising the soil PH.

Paul and Amanda O'Carroll
Gardeners, Rotherfield Park, Hants

DECOMPOSITION

When building a compost heap, add 1 in/2·5 cm of garden soil to every 12 in/30 cm of organic material. Sprinkle an additive such as Garotta with each layer and the composting will be improved by introducing the soil bacteria and nematodes required for decomposition.

Brian Davis
Garden consultant and lecturer

DON'T MAKE MOUNTAINS

Homemade John Innes-type composts are easily made by sterilizing the earth from mole hills. Two hours in the top oven of the Aga (200° C/400° F in an ordinary oven) using biscuit tins as containers does the trick.

A.W.A. Baker
Old Rectory Cottage, Berks

TOP OF THE HEAP

Stinging nettles are a must for any compost heap. Cut them down with a hedge trimmer, then run over them with a rotary mower set at top height. In the collecting bag there will be the equivalent of a fillet steak for the compost heap.

Patrick Braddell
Treasurer, Simon Weatherby Garden Trust,
Katharine House Hospice

FOR FREE

Free leaf mould for town gardens: collect fallen leaves in autumn, pack them in black plastic rubbish bags, and by the following autumn you will have quantities of leaf mould. N.B. Do not use the leaves of London plane trees, as they don't rot down.

Victoria Glendinning
Author and journalist

FROM COAL TO COMPOST

I've got an old concrete coal bunker, no longer needed in this age of central heating, but immovable. For years it remained a useless eyesore. Then I started to use it as a compost container and soon it spontaneously acquired its own flourishing colony of red worms. Nothing could be simpler. Throw all the household and kitchen waste into the top, shovel out very decent compost from the bottom. No other action needed. So now I've got a useful eyesore – and ivy is rapidly putting that right.

John Course,
Northern Editor, The Guardian

SOOTHING SITE

Compost heaps are rarely pretty, so why not improve the appearance with a planting of the the common comfrey, or a variety such as *Symphytum Grandiflorum* 'Hidcote Blue'? Occasionally chop the comfrey down and add it to the heap to aid decomposition.

Tom Stuart-Smith
Treasurer, Royal Horticultural Society

THE FLOWER GARDEN

FOR THE FORGETFUL

When new bulbs arrive in the autumn, if you have forgotten where you meant to put them, plant them in large plastic pots in well-draining compost. They can be planted out in the spring with no disturbance as their roots will hold the compost together. Alternatively, they can go, in their pots, into slightly larger display containers, any discrepancy in size being hidden by a covering of compost.

Mrs P. Liechti
Campden Cottage, Bucks

MARKED IN THE SAND

When planting bulbs in borders, add a fair amount of silver sand to the covering soil. When the borders are dug over, the presence of the bulbs will be obvious.

Lord Tombs
Honington Lodge, Warks

... Put sharpsand round the crowns of hostas – not only does it indicate their whereabouts in winter, but it is also a very effective slug-deterrent in spring.

Mrs John Makepeace
Parnham, Dorset

HOSTS FOR HOSTAS

I always plant snowdrops between and around hosta clumps. This protects the hosta's pointed buds as they come through and prevents them from getting trodden on while weeding. A further advantage is that the hosta leaves hide the snowdrops as they die away.

The Hon Mrs Payne
Scotlands, Berks

DOUBLE DELIGHT

Plant forms of *Geranium macrorrhizum* amongst snowdrops under flowering cherries. The top growth hides the dying leaves of the bulbs and provides a second period of bloom.

Mrs R. A. Boydell
The Garden House, W Yorks

SPRING TREAT

The little yellow *Iris danfordiae* deserves to be better known. It flowers in early February, is about 4 in/10 cm in height and grows well in rockeries or in the front of a border. It also does well in pots.

Dora Saint ('Miss Read')
Author

DIG DEEP

After their first flowering season the bulbs of *Iris danfordiae* have the most annoying habit of splitting up into lots of very small, non-flowering bulblets. Overcome this by planting them 4 in/10 cm deep.

Tony Venison
Gardening Editor, Country Life

29

DOUBLE DISPLAY

Underplant irises with Darwin hybrid tulips for a double display without using bedding plants. The tulips, flowering in May, will have died down sufficiently to be cleared away in time for the irises to flower in June.

Mrs David Hodges
Brook Cottage, Oxon

BURIED BASKETS

If you need to lift tulips after flowering, plant them in baskets made of wire-netting with a bent hazel rim. This ensures that none are left in the ground.

Mrs John Makepeace
Parnham, Dorset

ON THE SIDE

Plant *Fritillaria imperialis* (crown imperial) bulbs on their sides, to prevent water from collecting in their 'open' tops and rotting them.

Clay Jones
Chairman, Gardeners' Question Time

UNMIXED BLESSINGS

Don't mix early- and late-flowering daffodils together when planting – the later flowerers will be pushing up among the dead-heads of the early varieties and their impact will be lost.

Dr Stefan Buczacki
Gardening writer and broadcaster

TREBLE CHANCE

Daffodils in small town gardens are enchanting, but the dying foliage, so vital to the regeneration of the bulbs, is an eyesore in a small space. My remedy is to underplant a small variety of narcissus, ('Tête-à-Tête' is particularly suitable) with a group of hemerocallis. The fresh bright emerging leaves of the day lilies camouflage the fading foliage of the narcissus and the problem is solved. My choice of hemerocallis is usually the dwarf 'Stella d'Or' for its neat habit and long season of flower. This hard-working duo also works well in containers.

Susan Sharkey
Garden designer

A HOST OF CRIMSON DAFFODILS?

Scoop out the middle of a beetroot and insert a daffodil bulb in the resulting hole. Pack minced beetroot mixed with linseed oil round the bulb and plant it in the garden. Then, hey presto, when the daffodil flowers next spring it should be pink.

Bridie Pretejohn

COLOUR CODED

Crocuses planted in mixed groups tend to look messy – like a cake covered in hundreds and thousands. I like to see them planted in tight groups in single colours, following a serpentine line in rough grass well spaced out with specimen trees.

Jeremy Whitaker
Architectural and horticultural photographer

EXTEND THE SEASONS

To extend the season of interest with early flowering shrubs like forsythia, sow nasturtiums beneath. They will happily climb through the branches and brighten the summer months with their gold and scarlet flowers.

Sheena Crossley
Presenter, Get Gardening, *BBC Radio Wales*

A MIX FOR MINT

The large, flat-leaved mint is best, in my opinion, and for an elegant beginning to spring, plant creamy-white tulips amongst it.

Mrs R. J. C. Horan
Court End, Oxon

SPRING BEDDING

Aubretia, which is so easy to grow from seed, can be used very effectively for spring bedding as a colourful alternative to pansies and wallflowers.

Sheena Crossley
Presenter, Get Gardening, BBC Radio Wales

... Double or stock-flowered white arabis makes a marvellous plant for bedding out in the autumn, to flower the following spring. It provides a welcome change from polyanthus, forget-me-nots and wallflowers and is a pleasing setting for hyacinths or tulips. Four or five individual leafy rosettes, taken as cuttings with about 1½ – 2 in/3.8 cm – 5 cm of stem attached, can be bunched together and planted up to their lowest leaves in sandy soil outdoors. By the autumn they will be ready for planting out.

Tony Venison
Gardening Editor, Country Life

SEEN AND NOTED

1. An island bed planted with 'Nevada' roses, catmint, blue geraniums, alchemilla and pulmonaria. Planted very densely, the result is stunning.

2. Seen in early spring at St John's, Smith Square: a dense planting of white Lenten roses and white crocuses, underplanted with dwarf white vinca.

The Rt Hon John Biffen MP

COMPLIMENTARY

A very satisfactory study in pink and red can be achieved by underplanting the red-leaved *Photinia serrulata* 'Red Robin' with *Polygonum affine*, which has rosy-pink spikes in the autumn.

Jane Harris
Garden designer

A STRIKING CIRCLE

A lovely planting for a round island bed or large container: two or three plants of *Lavatera trimestris* 'Mont Blanc', surround with a circle of Nicotiana Domino Lime and around the outside, *Impatiens* 'Accent White'. These plants will grow into a spectacular cone of white and lime green in the summer.

The Lady Porchester
Highclere, Berks

AROMA THERAPY

For a layered border or island bed try using large groupings of herbs: lavender – *Lavandula spica* 'Hidcote' or 'Imperial Gem' – as edging with *Santolina neapolitana* as a backdrop. In between plant layers of white musk mallow, purple sage and red bergamot. Aromatic and attractive, even in the winter months.

Christine Lalumia
Keeper of Museum Services, Geffrye Museum, London

HIGH AND LOW

The pink *Arabis caucasica* 'Rosabella' looks lovely with the double tulip 'Angelique'.

Tony Venison
Gardening Editor, Country Life

WANDS AND FRONDS

Lavatera and artemisia are the best of friends, like a Persian cat with a bolt of silk. The slender silvery-grey fronds of the *Artemisia arborescens* entwine themselves to waist height among the arching wands of the palest pink *Lavatera thuringiaca* 'Barnsley' and with human intervention – it's like arranging a vase of flowers – becomes spectacular.

Eluned Price
Writer and broadcaster

MIXED BLESSINGS

I like the effect of under-planting with something of similar colour and overlapping flower period to prolong a garden picture. For example, 'Iceberg' roses look wonderful with white Japanese anemones growing into them, or old pink moss roses with pink ones. Lavender with catmint or campanula scrambling through is also a delight. The possibilities are endless.

Mrs Richard Springate
The Old Courthouse, Oxon

AFTERGLOW

For colour effect once rhododendrons and azaleas have flowered, grow white foxgloves amongst them. You can make sure the foxgloves are white by removing all the pink ones when they are over. Let the white foxgloves seed themselves naturally.

Elizabeth Banks
Hergest Croft Gardens, Heref & Worcs

COLOUR BAR

If you want only white foxgloves in your borders you can take out the red (wild) ones early on by looking at the base of their leaves – the red ones have a flush of pink on the outside rib.

Mrs Michael Todhunter
The Old Rectory, Berks

RAKING IT IN

The best-laid schemes, especially in a new garden, can get delayed and it can suddenly become too late for the planned permanent planting, although the new beds are prepared. For minimum cost you can have a blaze of colour. Rake the seeds of larkspur, clarkia, calendula, linum, nasturtium etc. gently into the new clean topsoil and the beds will be filled with bloom for most of the summer. And next summer, when the beds have been properly planted to plan, allow a few self-sown seeds to flower, filling the inevitable gaps between young plants.

Gillian Temple
Landscape designer and horticultural consultant

SOOTY

Soot, watered well in, will give sweet peas a much richer colour.

Judith Bannister
Head gardener, Kiftsgate Court, Glos

IN THE NEWS

My friend Barney, a pensioner from Middlesbrough, was lining his sweet pea trench with wet, shredded copies of the *Evening Gazette* when his grandson asked him what he was doing. 'Well,' he said, 'we spend so much money on papers I thought we should grow some.' On his next visit the little boy rushed out into the garden and was most disappointed to report, 'The papers aren't growing yet, Grandad!'

The Lady Gisborough

FISH BOOSTER

A very successful sweet pea grower told me that he always got all the waste products from his local fish shop and made a thick layer of them at the bottom of the trench when he was preparing it for planting, achieving excellent results – and no, the flowers don't smell of fish.

A. du Gard Pasley
Landscape architect

GROUND-COVER COVER

We planted the big-leaved golden ivy, *Hedera colchica* 'Dentata Variegata' as ground cover to brighten a yew-shaded border. By chance, we left a few campanulas in the bed; they have spread and in the summer their flowers shower over the ivy to give a haze of blue. When they are over and withered away we simply tear off the old stems and the ivy remains unscathed.

The Lady Wardington
Wardington Manor, Oxon

SHELTER BELT

Plants of doubtful hardiness can often be grown under an evergreen tree on the sunny side – but it is as important to provide good drainage as shelter from frost. Species which are kept dry by snow in their normal habitat, for example penstemons, can benefit in this position, as they can also on the sunny side of a hedge.

T.S B. Card
Vice-Provost's House, Eton College, Berks

STARVATION DIET

Wild flowers grow best in poor soil and therefore should never be fertilized.

Miriam Rothschild

HIT THE SPOT

Despair in finding a plant for a difficult spot, particularly if the soil is dry and alkaline, can usually be defeated with some sort of geranium.

The Lord Feversham
Duncombe Park, N Yorks

WHERE AND WHY

Never plant *Pupleurum fruticosum* near a window unless you want a room full of flies, but always plant an azara where you can smell it in February.

Paul Miles
Garden designer

VISITORS' VISIONS

Allium seedheads are valuable ingredients of an everlasting flower arrangement. They look wonderful in the border as well but are too fragile to withstand much weather. Now I harvest them as soon as the flower has faded, dry them off, and keep them for times when visitors are coming to the garden. Then I put them back in the ground, just for the day; nobody is any the wiser (except you, gentle reader) and this way they last much longer.

Andrew Lawson
Garden and landscape photographer

POTTED LILIES

Because our garden is heavy clay I plant liliums, alliums etc. in sunken pots with gravel at the base for good drainage and another layer on the top to prevent slug attack.

Mrs D.G. Jones
Rose Cottage, Bucks

OUT ON THE TILES

An old gardening friend told me many years ago that *Eremurus*, the fox-tail lily, likes to be planted with its curious starfish-shaped roots on a tile, which prevents the centre from rotting. It likes sun and lime too.

The Marchioness of Salisbury
Hatfield House, Herts

NAME-DROPPING

We have various lilies in herbaceous borders and every spring wonder anxiously where they are meant to come up, or if the deer have had them, or if we have killed them with mulch. Now it has occurred to me that I must put named labels on the stakes and leave them permanently in position.

Mrs E. R. Palmer
The Beacon, Bucks

WHERE AND WHEN

When planting large-flowered gladioli corms, put them in 6 in/15 cm deep. They will be less likely to suffer wind damage. Also, if their blooms are required for a special occasion, plant them 100–110 days before the event.

Clay Jones
Chairman, Gardeners' Question Time

CHANCE DOUBLE

I have four herbaceous borders which I love, despite the work they entail. I was therefore none too pleased when, one flaming June, the drought in Sussex reduced my favourite phlox to a seemingly autumnal display of withered foliage and faded flowers. Then I saw a gardening article which suggested planting the drought-resistant penstemon instead of phlox. I tried it last year and not only did it flower all summer, but the leaves remained on all last winter too. To crown it all, I failed to dig out every scrap of phlox, so if there is no drought this year I shall have penstemon *and* phlox – **the former** for reliability and elegance, the latter for scent and variety of colour.

The Countess of Longford

HAPPY PLACE

Don't always believe what you read in books. Most of them say you should never move peonies. I moved Kelways peonies after they had been unhappy in the border for at least six years and now they thrive in their new position. The secret is to find a place they will like, prepare the ground, dig the holes *before* digging the peonies up and plant immediately – and tell them they will be happy!

Mrs A. E. Pedder
Yeomans, Oxon

FISH MEAL

Having little success with a Chatham forget-me-not (*Myositidium hortensia*)? It's probably not receiving an interesting enough diet. It thrives on fish in any form – crab shells, mussels etc. and, in desperation, fish manure.

Mrs Charles Shepley-Cuthbert
Spring House, Northants

STOP GAP

Grow annual *Agrostemma githago* 'Milas' to plant out in the herbaceous border after the first flowering plants (erigerons, camassias etc.) are over. The agrostemma grows tall and fills the gaps with beautiful mauve flowers.

Anthea Gibson
Garden designer, Westwell Manor, Oxon

CUT AND COME AGAIN

Cut Michaelmas daisies down when the new growth is about 8 in/20 cm high. They will come again very quickly and be much sturdier when they flower.

Mrs John Montagu
Mapperton, Dorset

UNDER COVER

Don't place your chrysanthemums under cover until the buds have secured, otherwise they will only grow foliage.

John Higgs
Head gardener, Grey Gables, Borsetshire

HIGH COLOUR

To give height and late colour to your border grow buddleias like *Buddleia davidii* 'Dartmoor' or 'Black Knight' as small standards. Cut them back hard to a single stem. They take up no space and screen nothing in the spring but produce a fine display in late summer without staking.

John Sales
Chief Gardens Adviser, The National Trust

MAKE A STATEMENT

Make catmint a specimen statement in your border. Turn a wire hanging-basket upside down over the cut-down plant in winter and in the spring it will grow through the basket in a formal upright way instead of lying about on the ground.

Mrs Neil Petrie
Sulphur Wells, New Zealand

LIFE SUPPORT

As soon as the fragile-stemmed plants such as alstroemerias start showing, put canes around and cover them with sheep-wire. As the flowers grow, slide the wire up the canes for support.

The Lady Fanshawe

WIRED UP

An old wire coat-hanger pulled out square and put round a clump of herbaceous plants will make a good support if the hook is made to fit round the cane. If necessary, make a twist with pliers to the opposite corner to take another supporting cane.

Mrs Rosalind Squire
Tibby's Cottage, Bucks

PEA-STICKING

Here at Packwood we use the traditional method of pea-sticking to support herbaceous plants. In the winter we gather flexible sticks, branches and twigs so that we can stake early in the year. As the plants come through the supporting material they hide it completely and need no further support.

W. F. T Corrin
Packwood House, W Mid

NETTED

To avoid individual staking of plants in herbaceous borders, secure wide-mesh plastic netting to wooden stakes 2 ft/0·6 m high over the plants before they reach that height. The netting should cover the entire border; the plants will grow through it and stand up to wind and weather.

Robin Compton
Newby Hall, N Yorks

UNDERGROUND HIBERNATION

If you haven't the space to take your tender fuchsias indoors during the winter, try burying them. Before the frosts come, dig a hole deep enough to cover the plant completely, trim back any straggly growth, tip it out of its pot and put it, root first, into the hole. Cover it with earth and all that remains to be done is to mark the spot so that you can remember where it is when you come to dig it up in the spring. With a good wash and a new pot, it will have another happy summer.

Pamela Harper

GROUNDED

Most people take up dahlia tubers and store them inside during the winter months. In southern England they will survive through to the next year if left in the ground.

The Lady Cowdray
Cowdray Park, W. Sussex

UPSIDE DOWN

Use hanging baskets (if you don't need them for a winter display) as covers for tender plants, putting them over the plant stuffed with straw or bracken.

Mrs Denys Fraser
The Old Butchers Arms, Berks

42

DISTANCE LENDS ENCHANTMENT

Gardening is something I do not do, but once, when I felt I needed colour in the garden I bought large quantities of plastic flowers from Woolworths and stuck them in a flower-bed at the far end of the garden. They looked quite convincing from the living room window which was a long way away.

Claire Rayner
Agony aunt

ROSES, ROSES

If you are choosing roses and have any special problems – perhaps your soil is light or you are planting where roses have been grown before – I recommend hybrid musks as being the healthiest and most unfussy of the shrub roses. They have a delicious scent and are recurrent, and the clusters of flowers are soft in colour, most of them with a hint of apricot. My favourite is *Rosa* 'Buff Beauty'.

Anne Scott-James
Journalist

MAKE A BIGGER HOLE

Solve any problems you may have in growing roses, before you start by digging a hole several times bigger than the bush and quite deep. Fill the hole with well-rotted manure and plant the bush in it. Almost fill the hole with more manure and cover with soil. Remember to firm in well. In this way all our roses, particularly shrub roses, have been transformed.

David Brown
Regional Public Affairs Manager, The National Trust

MOVING

This may be good advice for anyone moving house. I had some old but particularly attractive climbing roses where I wanted to make a patio, so in November I cut them back to within 6 in/15 cm of the crown, dug them up, trimmed the roots and replanted them in the vegetable garden in a mixture of peat, compost and manure. They are now putting out shoots as though they have never been moved, and are ready to be put into a new climbing position.

Sir Edward Tomkins
Winslow Hall, Bucks

BANANA SPLIT

Save all your banana skins to put at the base of your roses when you plant them. As they decompose they provide the most wonderful nutriment for the flowers.

Lady Helen Smith

UNDER AND OVER

Underplant bush roses with species geranium or marjoram – golden marjoram beneath white or yellow roses and pink marjoram beneath pink roses.

Anthea Gibson
Garden designer, Westwell Manor, Oxon

COLOUR COMBINATIONS

Why not try a formal garden of pink, white and burgundy shrub roses underplanted with geraniums: *Geranium pratense* 'Johnson's Blue', and 'Kashmir White', *G. psilostemon* with the occasional plant of *Salvia sclarea turkestanica*?

Tom Stuart-Smith
Treasurer, Royal Horticultural Society

CLIMBING TREES

Plant climbing roses (*Rosa filipes* R. 'Kiftsgate', 'Rambling Rector', R. 'Constance Spry' etc.) up old fruit trees. The result in five years' time, as they reach the top, will be breathtaking.

The Hon. Mrs Hugh Astor
Folly Farm, Oxon

ANYONE FOR TENNIS?

Plant rambling roses, such as *Rosa* 'American Pillar', all along the plastic-coated wire netting of a tennis court to disguise it.

David Hicks
Interior decorator and garden designer

BEND OVER

When training climbing roses, bend the branches as far as possible horizontally before fixing them to a wall, trellis or pergola. This will result in many more flowers than if the roses had been allowed to climb vertically. We do this in the gardens here, where we have over two hundred varieties of old-fashioned roses, and so can guarantee that it really does work.

The Lady Ashcombe
Sudeley Castle, Glos

TIGHT TIES

I use the legs of old tights cut into strips to tie up the roses. They are much gentler than wire and cheaper than rose ties.

Prue Leith
Cookery writer

TOGETHERNESS

A rose looks wonderful with a clematis weaving through it, and vice versa. Plant them both in the same hole. The rose roots will keep the clematis cool – or so says Christopher Lloyd.

Mrs Moran Caplat

TASTY

Grow borage up through old-fashioned pink roses. The blue of the borage flowers intensifies the pink of the roses, while the rose gives support to the unruly borage plants. And the flower petals of both are handy to pick for salads, drinks and desserts.

Lesley Bremness
Herb grower and garden designer

GOOD ENOUGH TO EAT

Heavily scented rose petals taste wonderful. Make them into a delicious pink ice-cream by whirling them up in the food processor with a few drops of rose water in a basic ice-cream mixture. Serve it soon after it's been made; as with so many delicate ices the flavour fades in the freezer.

Carmen Basante
Cook

PAN OUT

Never let soil 'pan' in the rosebed. This can easily happen when you are cutting flowers, dead-heading or pruning, especially if it is wet at the time. The remedy is to use a sharp tool like a hoe or small spade to chip the surface over the bed – but be careful not to injure the stems while doing so.

Peter Harkness
Retired rosarian

BOOSTER

Epsom salts help roses in a wet season. One tablespoon per rose bush is enough to replace the minerals washed out of the soil.

Lady Georgina Coleridge
Freelance writer

MULCH, MULCH, MULCH

Roses can be kept happy if you provide a good mulch when the ground is wet in early spring; after pruning is the ideal time. The mulch can be composed of any organic material which provides a bulky application and some food. By doing this you can keep early weeds down and, even more important, keep the soil moist. Rose roots feed in solution, i.e. on dissolved material. You can give them the equivalent of a royal banquet but if moisture is not present they will sit and sorrow. If summer watering restrictions are likely to be imposed, the importance of mulching (and topping up) cannot be over-stated.

Peter Harkness
Retired rosarian

TEA-TIME

We had some moss roses which used to start the season looking marvellous, then when the buds should have opened they turned brown and mangy-looking. We were told by an expert that cold tea and tea leaves – not bags, unless you cut them open – should be put or poured on to the roots, and all would be well, and it was.

Mrs Dominic Cadbury
Shutford Manor, Oxon

48

PROTECTIVE MINT CARPET

Growing mint amongst old-fashioned roses provides ground cover and dissuades greenfly from landing on them.

Elizabeth Banks
Hergest Croft Gardens, Heref & Worcs

NEVER MIND THE SMELL

Wild garlic serves as a perfect ground cover under roses, smothering weeds and choosing to spread itself into shady places, and it deters greenfly as well. My son lives in Los Angeles in a house with a garden planted by Spaniards. They put garlic round the roses and my silly son ripped it out because he didn't like the pong. I bet his roses get greenfly now.

Alice Thomas Ellis
Author

SECOND TIME AROUND

To achieve a good second flowering on climbing roses, prune them in the autumn and then cut them back lightly after flowering in the spring.

Walter Upton
Head gardener, Friars Well, Oxon

SHEAR HEAVEN

There is really no need to dead-head vigorous ramblers such as *Rosa* 'Albertine' carefully once they have flowered. When you are tired of looking at the shrivelled petals, chop the long growth back with shears. Lots of time will be saved and the rose will be just as happy.

John Richardson
The Manor House, Lincs

ALL IN ONE

We prune all our hybrid tea and cluster roses as we do climbers and ramblers, in the autumn and early winter. We do a complete prune, removing all dead and discarded leaves from the beds at the same time. If diseases have been a problem we then spray both plants and soil with Tar Oil Winter Wash, Jeyes Fluid or Armillatox. If the soil is impacted or heavy we fork it over – the weathering over winter provides a beautiful tilth in the spring.

Brian Hutchinson
Head gardener, Castle Howard, N Yorks

KEEP CALM

Never go pruning when in a foul temper, or after a row with your spouse.

Gervase Jackson-Stops
The Menagerie, Northants

SPOT THE SUCKER

If in any doubt as to which shoot is a sucker and which the true rose, count the leaves. Suckers have seven leaves to a sprig and the true roses five.

Lord Montagu of Beaulieu
Palace House, Hants

CLIMBERS

WELL-WATERED

When planting a climber against a dry wall it's wise to plant, a few inches away from it, about a foot of pipe. Any water poured into the pipe will get directly to the roots, where it is needed.

Lady Anne Rasch
Heale Gardens, Wilts

COLD FEET

Never try to tease out the brittle roots of a clematis. Dig a large hole, add well-rotted compost and bonemeal, and when you plant the clematis, make sure the root-ball is at least 3 in/7·6 cm below the surface. Place a stone slab on the earth over the roots to keep them cool, and a handful of sulphate of potash popped under the stone in the spring will ensure a spectacular display of flowers.

Mrs J. Brooke
Overstroud Cottage, Bucks

SAFE-KEEPING

Use a short drainpipe to protect the delicate stem of a newly planted clematis from predators. Push the climber through the pipe and plant it so that the bottom of the pipe is in the soil and the dormant buds are protected from slugs and squirrels and can grow up through the pipe.

John Humphris
Chairman, Professional Gardeners Guild

TENDRIL SUPPORT

I put raspberry netting round tree trunks and stumps to help young clematis climb; it's almost invisible, rot proof, and soft enough not to damage young tendrils which often wilt on tarred or metal supports.

Lady Jocelyn
54 Burnfoot Avenue, London

TOUGH

Clematis need a vast amount of water and feeding to start with, and slugs will threaten new shoots, but once they are well established they are tough as old boots so don't worry too much.

Mrs John Boughey
NGS Hon. County Organizer, Northants

YEAR-ROUND INTEREST

A leggy climbing rose may be complemented by planting an early clematis such a *Clematis montana* 'Marjorie' (small cream and white flowers with pink edging) together with an ornamental grape. You will have flowers in the spring, leaves in summer, colour in autumn and delicate tracery in winter.

Mrs R. J. C. Horan
Court End, Oxon

VERSATILE TWINER

Humulus lupulus 'Aureus', the golden hop, is a wonderfully ornamental twining climber, grown for its lime-green palmate leaves carried on long stems. It will climb over arches with roses, or into trees, or – perhaps even better – cascade down a bank over other shrubs. The lemony-green leaves show up in garlands against any background and give a new interest when the flowering season is over. Being herbaceous, it can be cut away in winter.

Nada Jennett
Horticultural lecturer and adviser

SEXY

Sex is everything when choosing *Garrya elliptica*. This attractive shrub brightens a dark wall in winter with its long, pale catkins, but be sure to get a male plant – its catkins will be much longer.

The Lord Wardington
The Wardington Manor, Oxon

WISTERIA WISDOM

My wisteria refused to bloom after six years so I consulted a friend who worked at Wisley. He told me to cut it back to six buds in the autumn and then in March to cut it back to two buds on the new wood. Then to feed it. Lo and behold, the next year I had five flowers.

Ronnie Corbett
Comedian

... I have a magnificent mass of flowers on my white wisteria every May. I take tremendous trouble pruning it. I get at it every three weeks throughout the summer, cutting back to one or two buds whenever I see laterals starting from the stem, so that the energy of the plant goes into next year's flowers rather than long tendrils.

Jeremy Whitaker
Architectural and horticultural photographer

HURRY UP

Very often climbing plants are used to disguise an unsightly wall or building. Naturally growth never seems to be fast enough. However, one way we have found to encourage rapid coverage is to spray the actual wall with liquid fertilizer once a month. This works very successfully and the plants grow extremely quickly.

The Marquess of Northampton
Castle Ashby, Northants

LOOK TO THE FUTURE

If you wish to grow climbers but need to get to the fence or wall later for painting etc., secure some strong netting to the ground about 18 in/46 cm away from the base. Tie the other end to the top of the support and grow the climbers up it. The netting, plus plant, can then be laid down for maintenance.

Jill Thompson
Training co-ordinator, Horticultural Therapy

BLOOMING BROLLY

A circular washing-line makes an amazingly successful base for your favourite climber, transforming it into a floral umbrella in summer.

Mrs Neil Petrie
Sulphur Wells, New Zealand

STICK 'EM UP

To save fiddling with string or wire when training a young tendril of ivy or clematis to climb a trellis or wall, try Plasticine or Blu-Tack.

The Earl of Westmorland

UP THE WALL

It's lovely to grow climbing plants up the walls of a conservatory, but nails and wires can be unsightly. Why not line the walls with wire netting? It is virtually invisible when in place and, of course, makes a perfect base for any climber.

Rosemary Alexander
English Gardening School, Chelsea Physic Garden

CAMOUFLAGED

We have a stone house here and lots of walls in our garden. We find that pig wire makes an excellent support on which to grow clematis or any other climbers. We hang it in panels on the wall and, being the same colour, it can hardly be seen.

Countess Cairns
Bolehyde Manor, Wilts

TRIM FIGURES

Ivies are such versatile plants and invaluable for covering a boring wall or fence. To get them to grow faster and thicker, keep cutting them back. Wherever the tips are trimmed two or three strong shoots will sprout.

Mr R. J.Key
Ivy grower, Fibrex Nurseries

SPLASHED WITH LIGHT

If you have a fence you want to hide, first plant variegated ivies and then overplant with your chosen climbers. In this way, on the darkest winter days when the other things are leafless, your fence will seem splashed with sunlight.

Mrs Richard Springate
The Old Courthouse, Oxon

COMPLEMENTARY COLOURS

We have a great sprawling juniper nearly 15 ft/4·57 m long in one of our borders. Over it I am training two clematis, a pink *Clematis* × 'Comtesse de Bouchaud' and a blue *Clematis* × 'Perle d'Azur'. The two pinks contrast beautifully with the bluey-green foliage.

Mrs R. M. Cheney
9 The Butts, Northants

TREES AND SHRUBS

PERFECT PLEASURE

Few landscape features give as much pleasure as woodlands. They are places in which to stroll and sit, and a haven of wildlife, from foxes to nightingales. Changing with the season, they give year-long interest and beauty. Even a town garden can have a little copse or shelter belt.

Dame Sylvia Crowe
Landscape architect

TOGETHERNESS

A rare and charming combination: a copse of silver birch underplanted with variegated ground elder, giving a shimmering green and white effect.

Paul Miles
Garden designer

GET GROWING

There is much, often conflicting, advice on planting young trees, but generally they grow significantly better without competition from other plants – that is with at least 1¼ sq. yd/1 sq. m around the plant kept free from weeds, either by weeding or means of a tree mat. If the tree is planted in grass, long grass appears to be less competitive than short-mown grass, and can give some slight protection from rabbits.

J. B. E. Simmons
Curator, Royal Botanical Gardens, Kew, Surrey

BOXED IN

It is difficult to resist buying container-grown trees and shrubs when encountered, perhaps by chance, in the summer. For best results, wait until autumn before planting out and meanwhile, get a large cardboard box from the supermarket. Put it in a shaded place, cut it down to size, half fill it with good compost and, removing your new purchase from its container, plant it in the box, covering the roots with compost. Water it well through the summer and in the autumn, when you come to plant it in its appointed place, you will find a sizeable increase in root development.

D. Pycraft
Horticultural adviser, Royal Horticultural Society Gardens,
Wisley

THE RIGHT TIME

Despite what we are told, autumn is not necessarily the best time to plant shrubs. Be selective. Plants which could suffer during a hard winter are best planted in the spring. They will have a season's growth under their belts before facing their first winter.

Graham A. Pavey
Garden and landscape designer

AGAIN AND AGAIN AND AGAIN

Before planting your shrub make a suitable-sized hole for the plant concerned and fill the hole with water. Wait half an hour and fill the hole with water again. Wait *another* half hour and water again. *Then* put your plant in. It will be quite happy for weeks in dry weather without any more watering. This seems an awful nuisance at planting time but it really does work.

Lady Barbirolli
15a Buckland Crescent, London NW3

… Our planting method is similar to the above, in that we fill the hole with water before planting the shrub. But as it begins to drain away we put the plant in the hole and wait until the water has drained away completely before putting the soil around the plant and firming it in. Then we spread a dry mulch over the whole area. This prevents evaporation from around the roots and encourages them to grow downwards to where the water has drained.

Timothy Walker
Horti Praefectus, University of Oxford Botanic Garden

DROP THE DEAD DONKEY

I have been told that before planting a mulberry tree you should always put a dead donkey in the ground to fertilize the spot. I don't know whether it works or not, but when I planted a mulberry tree without a dead donkey, the mulberry tree died very soon.

Auberon Waugh
Editor, Literary Review

HIT THE SPOT

Watering trees planted on a steep bank can be a problem, as the water tends to run down the slope instead of soaking in round the roots. Plant a length of drainpipe end up next to the tree and water directly into the pipe. It will then be delivered straight to the roots.

Anna Pavord
Gardening correspondent, The Independent

SURVIVAL OF THE FITTEST

I recommend that any branches not looking well should be lopped off. A plant will always put its strength into its weakest elements, and the removal of these will enable the rest of the tree to flourish.

Lord Aberconway
Bodnant, Clwyd

SELF-DEFENCE

If rabbits or deer eat your azaleas or young rhodo-dendrons down almost to the roots, do not despair. Often the plant will become resistant to the depredations of these animals and will put out a poison to deter the predators and eventually flourish.

Edmund de Rothschild
Exbury, Hants

THE CRUELLEST CUT

Never prune walnut trees in winter; they will bleed for days or even weeks. Always prune them in full leaf.

Richard W. Green
Tree surgeon

FORGO THE FLOWERS

Shrubs with silver foliage among the flowers in a border look wonderful – but some such as santolinas, *Senecio laxifolius* 'Sunshine', *Phlomis fruticosa* and *Ruta graveolens* have hard yellow flowers which do not look so good when in bloom. Keep the plants spherical and reduce flowering by clipping them back 6–9 in/15–23 cm in the spring.

Nada Jennett
Horticultural lecturer and adviser

LIVING SOUVENIRS

When I was on holiday in Hungary I picked up some chestnuts which had fallen by the roadside. I took them back to my home in Vermont and planted them, and now I have several strong chestnut saplings, a living reminder of a happy trip.

Stephen Massey

AN OLD FRIEND

If you have an old tree to which you are senti-mentally attached and which has to be felled, ask your local nurseryman to take a graft bud cutting before cutting it down. When he has propagated it you will be able to replace the old tree with its clone.

Richard W. Green
Tree surgeon

RESCUE WORK

There may be a chance to save a tired old tree by following the advice of a French lady – it worked on our walnut of a hundred years or so. Peg out a circle (more or less) underneath the ends of the tree's branches. Make holes, 2–3 in/6–7·5 cm across and 6–8 in/15–17 cm deep, 12–18 in/30–46 cm either side of the circle. They will add up to about a hundred holes. In each, put a handful of granular fertilizer. Fill them up with compost and pray for heavy rain. All the above ensures that the young root ends are stimulated.

The Earl of Perth
Stobhall by Perth

EVERLASTING CHRISTMAS TREES

A living Christmas tree is a joy, but it will almost certainly die when planted out after the holiday. Avoid this sad demise by getting a Norway spruce (which is what a Christmas tree is) in a pot and planting it, pot and all, in the garden to be lifted when you need it. Remember to water it well all the year round. You won't have to spend a lot of money on a new tree every year and, an added bonus, it won't drop needles.

Nicholas Turrell
Horticulturist and journalist

UNDERSKIRTS

Trees that are grown in lawns need the grass cut around them. This is especially true of the hummock-forming Japanese maples with lacy skirts that come right down to the lawn. The problem is how to cut the grass without damaging the trees. A crook sees to this: a long stick with a fork at the end which will prop up a branch while you cut underneath.

Joan Loraine
Garden designer

WINTER BUYS

When you are planning to buy trees and shrubs, visit nurseries and garden centres in November and December. It is then that the best plants are available, the retail outlets having restocked over this period from the growers.

Clive Jones
Founder of the Quercy Horticultural Association

KISSING TIME

If you want to get mistletoe to grow on your apple trees, save the berries until March, when they'll be really ripe. Then make a nick in the bark on the underside of the branch, and insert the sticky seed.

Judy Challoner
Head of Horticulture, Usk College, Gwent

WEBBED

If the leaves of your young magnolias look like cobwebs, buy yourself some slug pellets.

Sir Arscott Molesworth-St-Aubyn
Pencarrow, Cornwall

RHODO TREES

Nothing is uglier out of season than big heavy *Rhododendron ponticum*, but it is possible to turn quite large bushes into trees. Prune the branches until you have one main stem and after several seasons – it's not a process that can be hurried – you will have a tree. This makes garden planning on a large scale particularly exciting, as you can combine a canopy of colour above with vistas on all sides.

Countess Michalowska
House-in-the-Wood, Hants

64

WAIT AND SEE

When a tree or shrub looks as if it has died in the winter, either blasted by frost or broken by a falling branch, resist the temptation to dig it up and plant something new. More often than not, just when you have given up all hope of its survival it will sprout new shoots and be as strong as ever the following year.

The Rt Hon Michael Heseltine MP

SELECTIVE FEEDERS

Tree peonies are not at all happy with manure but love compost and bonemeal. Put both on in October, likewise with camellias.

The Marchioness of Salisbury
Hatfield House, Herts

GOLDEN RETURNS

The golden mock orange (*Philadelphus coronarius* 'Aureus') has only one drawback: when it is situated in full sun – where it looks wonderful – the leaves at the end of the branches go brown. I cut these off, sacrificing flowers but being rewarded by new golden growth during the summer.

The Lady Remnant
Bear Ash, Berks

PASTE IT

Moving shrubs in the summer is often difficult because the leaves flag and die easily. Water the plant well and then spray it with diluted wallpaper paste (non-fungicide). This helps reduce water loss and so will aid its survival.

Richard W. Green
Tree surgeon

PAINLESS TRANSPLANT

When we transplanted a tree at the wrong time of the year we knew we needed to keep the roots well watered. We cut the bottom off a 1 gal/4·5 l mineral-water container and sank it, spout down, into the ground beside the newly planted tree. We simply filled it with water every day and the tree flourishes.

Penny Kitchen
Editor, Home and Country

CLEAN SHEETS

A new shrub bed can be kept clean by covering it, once it is weed free, with heavy-duty black plastic sheeting. Planting can be done through slits in the plastic which should then be covered with gravel, bark or mulch. The bed will hold moisture and remain weedless.

John Humphris
Chairman, Professional Gardeners Guild

MUSHROOM MULCH

Mushroom compost is cheap to buy from mushroom farms and is a wonderful mulch for the shrub border – with the added bonus of a crop of mushrooms. But it is best not used around acid-loving plants as it contains lime.

Sheena Crossley
Presenter, Get Gardening BBC *Radio Wales*

TENDER CARE

Yew hedging can be encouraged to grow at least 9–12 in/23–30 cm annually during its first years, but it is essential to prepare the ground well with rotted manure and to keep it watered and fertilized until the hedge reaches the required height. The myth that yew hedges are slow is simply because they are so often planted and left to fend for themselves.

Mrs Phillip Trevor-Jones
Preen Manor, Shrops

... I feed yew hedges annually in the spring with Dried Blood at the rate of 4 oz/125 g to 1 sq. yd/0·8 sq. m of hedge run. It not only speeds up growth and keeps the hedge dark green but also can be used to rejuvenate old established hedges.

Brian Davis
Garden consultant and lecturer

THE A LINE

Don't cut the tops of young yews until they have reached the height you want (disregard the experts who give dire warnings that they will be thin at the bottom if you don't – they won't be). However, clip the sides quite hard, so forcing all growth to go sideways and upwards, and in an A shape to keep the hedge well furnished lower down.

The Marchioness of Salisbury
Hatfield House, Herts

WASTE NOT, WANT NOT

Anyone with a considerable amount of yew hedging can actually sell the clippings. They are currently in demand for use in cancer research and reasonable prices are being paid. Write for more details to Mr John Cook, Old House Farm, Stubbs Walden, Doncaster, DN6 9BU.

C. H. Bagot
Levens Hall, Cumbria

SIDE BY SIDE

An overgrown yew hedge can be knocked back into shape quite easily. Do it now, don't put it off. Only do one side and the top this year and do the other side next year so that the plant doesn't have too much of a shock. The hedge may look rather untidy for a year or two – which is why I say don't dither about – but I guarantee that it will respond to treatment.

Brian Hutchinson
Head gardener, Castle Howard, N Yorks

KINDEST CUT

Always clip back to last year's cut – if the hedge gets even an inch wider every year it will be two feet wider in twelve years' time and quite unmanageable in twenty.

Jeremy Whitaker
Architectural and horticultural photographer

SECRET PASSAGE

I have planted a cypress hedge to be a wind break, but since it separates one part of the garden from another, I needed to make a gap in it. It is a thick hedge and so it has been possible to cut the gap diagonally, in the opposite direction to the prevailing wind. Now, viewed from practically anywhere the hedge seems to be solid but allows passage from one side to the other.

Graham Rose
Gardening correspondent, Sunday Times

GATHER THY CLIPPINGS

Commandeer an old bed sheet from your wife (or, if you *are* a wife, take the law into your own hands) and lay it over any plants that are alongside a hedge while it is being clipped. This means that you can instantly gather up and dispose of the clippings instead of hand-picking them from beds and borders below. The sheet is also light enough to do adjacent greenery little damage when laid on top.

Alan Titchmarsh
Gardener and broadcaster

... A large cardboard box placed at one's feet while clipping will collect most of the mess if you move it along as you progress down the hedge.

Tom Cochrane
Plumber

QUICK AND EASY

Clip *Crataegus monogyna* (common hawthorn) to make topiary because it grows fairly fast and looks equally good in winter and summer.

David Hicks
Interior decorator and garden designer

WHEN IT'S WET

Always cut box after a shower of rain. Never cut it when it's dry.

Paul and Amanda O'Carroll
Gardeners, Rotherfield Park, Hants

DON'T LOOK BACK

When cutting a hedge always walk backwards (carefully) so that you can see what you have cut and keep a straight side and a level top.

J. M. Marshall
Gardens adviser, The National Trust

SAFE CLIPPING

One of the trickiest and most dangerous jobs in the garden is clipping a tall hedge of immature trees. The problem is that the main stems of the trees are not strong enough to support the ladder needed to clip the top areas of canopy. A simple and effective answer is to rope firmly a long (8ft/2·5 m) stout board across the top of the ladder so that the board is flat against the ladder. When the board is laid across the top sections of the trees the weight of the ladder and anyone on it will be supported by several main stems and clipping can be carried out in safety.

Graham Rose
Gardening correspondent, Sunday Times

BIRD SANCTUARY

As herb gardens are now becoming more ornamental, why not surround yours with a birds'
hedge *à la française*? The idea is to provide birds
with food, shelter and safety. For instance, a yew at

each end with hornbeams, hazel, hawthorn, copper beech (for colour) and lime as well as roses with hips etc. Plant the hedge closely with the sides left rough and kept to a height of 5 ft/1·5 m, and trim it only after the berries have been eaten. It also looks very pretty.

Mrs Charles Shepley-Cuthbert
Spring House, Northants

NETTLED

If you wish to plant a tree in a field, search out a strong patch of nettles, the markers of rich soil. By July they will have done their growing and, if the summer should prove hot and dry, will not compete for water and will shade the tree's roots. No need to ring with chemicals, no need to water.

Lady Cripps
Fox House, Filkins, Oxon

THE KITCHEN GARDEN

THE KITCHEN GARDEN

If you want to prepare a vegetable patch from a weed-ridden site, you will hardly have to do anything other than wait if you follow this course of action. Spread it with well-rotted farmyard manure to a depth of about 6 in/15 cm. Cover it with black polythene secured with stones and planks. Leave it for a year, from one spring to another, and the ground will be ready for planting.

Roddy Llewellyn
Gardening correspondent, Mail on Sunday

IN CLOVER

Use red or white flowering clover as a green manure if you are fallowing part of the kitchen garden. At the end of the season rotovate it thoroughly or spray it with weed killer.

Elizabeth Banks
Hergest Croft Gardens, Heref & Worcs

SPACE SAVERS

If you are short of space, make your own grow-bags. The ones you can buy are not only expensive but also heavy, so use up old plastic carrier bags instead. Fill them with any compost you can find and plant your tomato seedlings, one in each bag. They will be light enough to move around to sunnier corners.

Mrs Marion Henderson
NGS Hon.County Organizer, Berks

INSULATION

Tomatoes planted early in grow-bags in a cold greenhouse can be affected by cold when they are placed directly on the floor. We have used double layers of bubble plastic as an insulator between floor and bag with great success but now we find that polystyrene pot-plant trays which florists discard are even better.

Brian Hutchinson
Head gardener, Castle Howard, N Yorks

A LITTLE BIT OF FLUFF

Don't waste your Hoover fluff – it can make all the difference to the colour and quality of your tomatoes. Once the plants are well established apply regular amounts of fluff at the base of the tomato, adding a little water to keep it in place. It's the minerals in the fluff that give them a terrific boost. Every now and then add a dessert-spoon of sugar to your watering-can, which guarantees really sweet tomatoes.

Audrey Whiting
Journalist

BEANO

When my french beans are finished I demolish
them with the Flymo. It chops the plants into tiny
pieces and they are then easily dug into the
ground *in situ*. Sadly, the same cannot be said for
runner beans, which seem to be made of sterner
stuff.

Neil Gadsby
Director, Katharine House Hospice

ALL WASHED UP

Caterpillars love cabbages, and what a bore they
are! Watch out for the first signs of the pests and
dissolve several handfuls of salt in a little hot
water. Dilute with cold water and sprinkle it on
the young cabbage plants. The caterpillars will be
washed away and, revolted by the salt, will not
return.

Margaret Bülle

CLUB ROOT

If your soil is infested with club root which ruins
your hopes for brassicas, take heart. Sow seeds in
sweet-pea tubes and plant them out in the garden
with a 2 in/6 cm piece of rhubarb snuggling next
to each one.

Mrs Edward Crutchley

TRENCH WARFARE

To ensure a successful broad bean crop, dig a deep
trench in the late autumn before the frosts come.
Line it with well-spread-out manure and then a
fairly deep layer of crumpled newspaper. Plant your
beans in seed boxes in the greenhouse in early

December and replant in your prepared trench in early spring, about 12 in/30 cm apart, and firm well in.

Mrs Kay Goddard

BEAN BANE

Black fly are the bane of broad beans. A simple way to help deter them is to plant garlic cloves amongst the bean plants.

The Lady Burnham
Hall Barn, Bucks

TIP OFF

Newly planted onion sets are often pulled out by birds in search of food. By trimming off the small dry tips before planting out, this problem can be solved.

Ian Cooke
Head gardener, Ascott, Bucks

FLY AWAY

If you plant french marigolds alongside your rows of carrots, not only will they lend a splash of colour, they will also keep away the aphids.

Jeremy Nichols
Headmaster, Stowe School, Bucks

KING-SIZE BEDS

Individual rows of carrots can be fiddly and time-consuming. A good alternative, particularly in smaller kitchen gardens, is to create wide beds. Prepare a fine tilth some 2 ft/0·6 m wide and broadcast the seed in the usual fashion, i.e. very finely, ideally well mixed with sand at the rate of 1 pt/600 ml of sand per half-packet of seed. Rake over gently, water, and wait for a thicket to grow. Outside carrots will grow faster because of the extra light, thus giving you a successional crop as you pick from the outside towards the middle, as well as saving space and weeding time.

Michael O'Halloran
Littleworth Farm, Bucks

DEATH ON REFLECTION

If you put a few pieces of mirror in your carrot bed, when the female carrot fly comes to lay her eggs she will see her reflection in the glass and, thinking it is another female, will attack it and stun herself. Then you just go round picking off the corpses.

A. E. H. Heber Percy
Hodnet Hall, Shrops

LOO-ROLLED LEEKS

Long-stemmed autumn leeks don't have to be earthed up or transplanted over-deeply. In summer, simply put the core of a used lavatory roll over the plant until it touches the soil, fill up with just a handful of fine earth or peat and keep repeating the process until the plant stops growing. This method works particularly well on heavy or clay soils.

Michael O'Halloran
Littleworth Farm, Bucks

DOUBLE CROP

Sow parsnip seeds 9 in/23 cm apart with radishes in between. The radishes come up first, so you will be able to see where the parsnips will be, and the parsnips will not need thinning after the radishes have been harvested. I've done this for years; double cropping is great in a small patch and if one grows several rows it's even easier.

Mrs G. E. Davey-Turner
The Old Manor House, Northants

MARROW ARCHES

Try to grow trailing marrows in a more decorative way by training them up arches; they will hang down dramatically and be decorative and eye-catching. Ornamental gourds grown like this are even more exciting with their range of shapes.

Rosemary Verey
Gardening adviser and writer

ARTFUL ASPARAGUS

Between our bungalow wall and the surrounding path we have a strip of small stones, under which is sand and sludgy soil. We have taken some asparagus plants from the row in our vegetable plot and planted them in this poor medium, where they are producing fabulous spears of great size and delicate flavour. I neither feed nor water them and wonder what the experts have to say about this totally unorthodox way of growing this king of vegetables.

Mrs R.M.Cheney
9 The Butts, Northants

A CERTAINTY

Here's an easy way to remember when to stop cutting asparagus. Ascot Week. When that starts, it's time to stop.

Lady Scott
Rotherfield Park, Hants

SPRING SPINACH

Sow spinach in September; it will germinate, overwinter, and you can be picking from mid-March.

Mrs S. Freund
Swinbrook Manor Farm, Oxon

PEA PROTECTION

Mice are often a problem, eating peas before they have germinated. Cover the drill with a sheet of wide-mesh chicken wire, creased along the centre to make a tent shape. As the peas grow up, the chicken wire acts as a support and you won't need to do any further staking. This method, of course, only works with fairly strong varieties.

Anna Pavord
Gardening correspondent, The Independent

PRICKLY PROTECTION

When planting peas, surround them, below the surface, with holly leaves. When mice try to dig up the peas they prick themselves and are put off.

Martin Lane Fox
Hazelby House, Berks

STRANDED

To stop birds pecking pea seedlings or having dust

78

baths among them, stretch strands of black cotton
1 in/2.5 cm above the soil along the length of the
row. When the bird touches it with its wing, it
can't see the cotton against the soil and is fright-
ened away.

Mrs Andrea Bates

NETTING TENT

To protect rows of vegetable seeds from birds, cut
the required lengths from a roll of 3 ft/1 m wide
wire netting. Fold the lengths down the middle to
form a tent, the base of which can be pulled out to
accommodate any row width up to two feet. I use
1¼ in/3 cm netting.

Desmond Day
Editor, The Horticulturist

IN THE NEWS

If you garden on light soil, and are worried about
summer drought, line the bottom of your sweet
pea, potato and runner bean trenches with a layer
of shredded newspaper. Before sowing or planting
soak the paper well and then cover it with a little
soil. Newspaper retains moisture well and is
perfectly biodegradable.

Ursula Buchan
Gardening journalist

INSTANT SCREENING

Fix wheels on to a long narrow box such as a
window box (we use a wooden one) and plant it
with runner beans. When they grow up you have
an attractive movable screen.

Jessica Otley

SPUD DOUBLE

Gardeners who have the space to plant potato tubers in June will be enjoying new potatoes again in August and September.

Albert Reed
Head gardener, Swyncombe House, Oxon

SNAKES ON GUARD

Pieces of hosepipe about a yard long put among young lettuces will keep pigeons away. Apparently the birds think they are snakes. And, I'm told, cats keep away too.

Bill Ward
Part-time gardener

SALT FOR STARTERS

Salt sprinkled in the row before sowing beetroot will help to get it going.

Michael Mander

SAGACIOUS

A sage plant becomes woody and leggy if it is not trimmed regularly. To rejuvenate it, if this occurs, dig it up and plant it deeper.

Mrs Alan Meigh
Fishponds Farm House, Berks

SEGREGATION

It is a great delight to have a herb garden with a wide variety in it, particularly different kinds of mint. However, it is a particular problem to confine them, otherwise eventually the mint, lemon balm, tarragon etc. – all of which spread underground – will tend to take over. If you sink a series of wooden boards underground, about 12–15 in/30–38 cm deep, with their edges just level with the ground, and corners carefully joined, the herbs will be confined. Alternatively, use half a barrel sunk into the earth with either holes drilled into the bottom, or the base cut off completely.

The Earl of Bradford
Weston Park, Shrops

DOUBLE DELIGHT

The leaf of the sweet rocket (*Eruca sativa*) grown in a pot on the window ledge provides a tangy addition to a green salad and a flower that attracts hummingbird moths. Either will add charm to your day.

John Miller

HANDY HERBS

Buy three large clay plant pots and position them outside your back door. Plant up one with mint, one with basil and one with parsley, all in the spring, and you will have handy herbs for the rest of the summer without getting your feet wet.

Alan Titchmarsh
Gardening writer and broadcaster

MOTH BAGS

An aromatic moth deterrent:

    2 parts powdered mint leaves
    2 parts powdered rosemary leaves
    1 part sifted thyme
    1 part dried tansy leaves
    1 part powdered cloves.

Mix together and place in muslin bags.

Lady Scott
Rotherfield Park, Hants

81

TRIED AND TRUE

The old-fashioned varieties of strawberries are by far the best, and the tastiest. Why not propagate your own by pegging down runners into 3½ in/ 9 cm pots of compost so that you can provide plants to make a new bed next year?

Mr and Mrs Tom Forest
Keepers Cottage, Ambridge, Borsetshire

PINING FOR STRAWBERRIES

If you have access to lots of pine needles (we sweep ours off the tennis court) mulch the strawberry bed very thickly with them. They keep down the weeds and slugs hate them, but the strawberries seem to love them. We have quite acid soil already but since I have been putting down pine needles our crop has been really excellent.

Mrs P. Bradly
Whiteknights, Berks

COVER UP

Wild strawberries can be grown in great profusion as ground cover. They seem to thrive in sun or shade, spreading in a most obliging way, smothering weeds and delivering a delicious harvest as well. It's disastrous to plant them under roses, though: you get torn to bits while you're picking.

The Hon. W. S. Pease

STAND UP STRAIGHT

Seeing fraises de bois in several gardens recently reminded me of my father's ingenious notion of digging a wide, deepish trench alongside the bed, thereby ensuring upright picking, manuring *et al.*

Mrs Charles Shepley-Cuthbert
Spring House, Northants

ON THE SQUARE

Grow strawberry varieties in blocks – for example, in a four-row square – so that you can use the runners growing along the outer edge to replace the first row and keep the rotation going.

Elizabeth Banks
Hergest Croft Gardens, Heref & Worcs

TOAD ON GUARD

A toad put into a strawberry bed during fruiting will keep it slug-free.

Mary Goldring
Freelance economist

BARBED SUPPORT

Raspberries and barbed wire do not seem to go together but in fact, if the latter is used instead of ordinary wire the barbs will keep the canes from slipping about and so make for less tangled plants.

Kit Hall
Ashford Manor, Shrops

HAPPY FAMILIES

My wife tells me that if you spread grass cuttings thickly between raspberry canes it acts as a very good mulch and keeps down the weeds. My own advice, however, to anyone who has a garden but hates gardening – like me – is to marry someone who loves it, as fortunately I did.

John Timpson
Writer and broadcaster

TRY BEFORE YOU BUY

Catalogue descriptions for soft fruits may tell you about the size, yield and habit of plants, but can't possibly describe their most important ingredient – flavour. If you're planning to plant raspberries, strawberries or other fruits, visit your local pick-your-own first. Try varieties regularly through the summer, ask for the names of the ones you like best and plant these. If they grow well locally they should do well in your soil and situation too.

Alan Pasco
Editor, BBC Gardeners' World Magazine

HEN-PECKED

Chickens, let into a permanent fruit cage once the fruit is picked, will destroy insects and their eggs, do the weeding, scarify and manure and enormously enjoy themselves.

Mary Goldring
Freelance economist

PICK AND PRUNE

When harvesting blackcurrants, prune the bushes at the same time. Cut off the fruiting branches and strip them of their fruit while sitting in the sun.

Mrs Nigel Viney
The Post House, Bucks

THEN AND NOW

Hang up phials of sugared or honeyed water to catch the wasps and flies which come to eat choice wall fruit. Besides the bottles of sweetened water, let also some small bags, made of thin crêpe or gauze, just so large as to contain one bunch of fruit, be put over the finest and ripest of the bunches of grapes. This will effectually keep off the insects and also the birds. The latter you may also keep from the fruit by hanging up scarecrows of feathers or discharging gun or pistol, but the most certain method to preserve some of the finest bunches of fruit from all devourers is to bag them as above directed.

The Gardeners' Calendar 1800

In 1993 this advice may be followed by the use of nylon stockings, a perfect substitute for bags of 'thin crêpe or gauze' and less hazardous than discharging gun or pistol.

Rosemary Nicholson
Founder of the Museum of Garden History, Lambeth

WASP WATCH

Tie plastic bags round peaches on the tree before they are ripe, having first punctured holes in the bags. The fruit will be protected from wasp attack, ripen quickly and be extra juicy.

Mrs Francis Sitwell
Weston Hall, Northants

A PEACH OF AN IDEA

Our two splendid peach trees, espaliered against a sunny wall, are blighted by leaf curl and squirrels. We've beaten them both by fastening plastic sheeting from wooden battens at the top of the wall down to the ground. These sheets stand about 6 in/15 cm away from the branches and protect the leaves from curl and the fruit from squirrels.

Lady Sophia Schilizzi
The Old Vicarage, Northants

PERFECT POLLINATION

If you have a solitary fruit tree that needs a pollinator, hang sprigs of blossom from another tree in two or three jars among the branches. This saves buying another tree.

Lord Montagu of Beaulieu
Palace House, Hants

SUPPORT FROM ABOVE

Melons tend to be too heavy for the strength of their stalks. Save the nets in which oranges are often bought and put the melons in them, attaching them to the branch above. As the fruit grows, the nets will expand and the weight will be taken by the branch.

Mrs Adrian Wield
Tysoe Manor, Warks

FRUIT SAVERS

Avoid late frost damage to fragile fruit trees by covering them with bubble plastic.

Mr and Mrs Robert Snell
Ambridge Hall, Borsetshire

HENCE MOUTON CADET?

I have always believed that grape vines do best when their roots can feed upon the carcass of a dead sheep, because this was told to me as a boy by the family gardener who was with us for thirty years and whose judgement I trusted implicitly.

The Lord Palumbo
Bagnor Manor, Berks

POTS, PATHS AND PATIOS

INTERLININGS

I like clay pots for plants and usually the larger the better. But, attractive as they are, they dry out much faster than plastic ones. So if you decide to use them, always line them with a plastic bag or sheet before planting up.

The Rt Hon Kenneth Clarke MP

… I like to line the terracotta pots with several layers of wet newspaper before use.

Helen Morling
Head gardener, Pettifers, Oxon

… I line my terracotta pots with bubble-wrap – on the sides only. It gives perfect insulation in very hot weather, and conserves moisture in the soil.

Spindrift Al Swaidi
Garden designer

ONE FOR THE POT

Tea-bags make good substitutes for broken crocks in the base of terracotta or plastic plant pots (used tea-bags, I hasten to add).

Katie Boyle
TV and radio personality

LITTLE IRRIGATORS

Sink little flower pots, empty, in your summer bedding tubs so that when you water they fill up and act as little reservoirs, gradually letting water into the pot.

Mrs John Makepeace
Parnham, Dorset

PEBBLE DASH

When growing plants in pots I cover the surface with gravel or small pebbles. This stops consolidation of soil when watering, reduces evaporation and keeps down weeds. The pebbles look good with plants such as cordylines and yuccas – and a thick layer helps to stop the soil freezing in winter.

Mrs A. F. Boydell
The Garden House, W Yorks

FAIR SHARES

It can be difficult to water all the plants in a strawberry planter; the ones at the top don't get their fair share. Now I have inserted, down the centre of the pot, a length of 1½ in/4 cm plastic waste pipe with holes drilled in it. I pour water in at the top and this irrigates the plants at all depths.

Ray Cherry
Master builder

HERBAL REMEDY

Containers standing in saucers on a roof garden or patio can be kept from drying out in summer by planting herbs or small flowers in the saucer.

Lady Georgina Coleridge
Freelance writer

GROW AN OVERCOAT

One of the disadvantages of growing specimen plants in large containers is they are too heavy to move under cover in winter. Overcome some of the dangers by planting trailing ivies around the edge of the pot to form an evergreen insulating blanket. Go for ivies with attractive variegated leaves and add spring bulbs to give another layer of interest. This simple idea works particularly well with figs which like to have their roots restricted but would not like them frozen. Ivies can also be used to hide a less-than-beautiful container.

Rosie Atkins
Gardening writer and broadcaster

ROYAL SHOW

I grow Regal pelargoniums in pots. In August, when three- or four-year-old plants have finished flowering I cut them back to 5–6 in/12·5–15 cm just above a node. I leave them outside in a sunny spot until October, when I take them into the greenhouse (which I keep at 45–50° F/7–10° C in winter). By Easter they have bushed out well. Pinch out some shoots to make them even bushier and they will be in full flower in May or June.

Sir Edward Tomkins
Winslow Hall, Bucks

PELARGONIUM TOPIARY

Insert a 4 ft/1·2 cm cane into a terracotta pot and attach a circular piece of bamboo or wire to the top of it, flat against the cane. Plant the pot with a single-stem zonal pelargonium, tying it in and removing all the side shoots. It will make an innovative and eye-catching standard. Make two pots and place them on either side of a doorway.

Richard Rosenfeld
Journalist

TREBLE CHANCE

When you plant bulbs in containers, whether for the house or for outdoors, you can provide a long display of flowers by planting in layers. I start with a layer of tulips 6–8 in/15–20 cm deep, alternating early ones with the later parrot or peony-flowered varieties. I cover these with a layer of compost, then a layer of narcissi to flower from the end of March into April. Into the top layer go crocus or *Iris reticulata* to start the season. As each lot finishes flowering, cut out the dead stem. The foliage will be hidden by the leaves of the next crop.

Jane Fearnley-Whittingstall
Landscape and garden designer

COUNTER INVASION

Some plants are too dangerous to let loose in the border. *Convolvulus althaeoides*, with its 1 in/2·5 cm wide pink trumpet flowers and trailing silvery foliage, is such a one. Imprison it in a strawberry pot and be rewarded with a disciplined cloud of pink and silver from July to the frosts.

Mrs David Hodges
Brook Cottage, Oxon

91

VARIETY PERFORMANCE

A clump of hostas in the middle of a large pot edged with variegated ivy makes an attractive and labour-saving permanent planting.

Mrs M. Ribton

WATER, WATER

Hanging baskets should be watered at least twice a day so that all levels of the soil remain well soaked. Once any part of the basket dries out it is very difficult to water sufficiently again and the roots of the plant will have died.

The Lady Porchester
Highclere, Berks

DOUBLE DUTY

Don't waste water. Place planted-up tubs or pots underneath hanging baskets so that they get a free drink every time you water the containers above.

Lynne V. Barber
Editor, Garden Answers

BOTTLE IN A BASKET

Keep hanging baskets from drying out quickly in hot weather by giving them their own individual reservoirs. Make some pinholes in the base of a plastic soft drinks bottle, and then sink it into the middle of the hanging basket, concealed amongst the plants. Simply top it up every few days.

Sue Phillips
Gardening writer and consultant

INSTANT REPLACEMENTS

In spite of the best care and attention, some of our hanging baskets wither. Now we keep extra ones permanently planted in the greenhouse and spare ourselves angst and aggravation by simply replacing the dead ones.

Lady Broakes
Checkendon Court, Oxon

DIMPLED BOTTOMS

Any bottle with a dimple in the bottom will make an unusual hanging flower container. Tap the dimple with a hammer – it will give way quite easily – and fill the bottle through the resulting hole with compost. Plant a geranium cutting in it. Keep the bottle well watered, neck down in soil to keep it upright, until the plant is well rooted. Then tie string round the bottle neck and hang it up. The geranium, provided it is not of the trailing variety, will turn upwards towards the sun enclosing the bottle.

Peter Bullen
Bramble Tye, Bucks

FOCAL POINT

Where a quick result and inexpensive focal point are needed, grow an ivy pillar. Five scaffold poles, placed in a circle and tied together firmly at the top with wire, will support three or four variegated ivies which will quickly grow up and smother the structure. It's important to keep the column clipped to preserve its slim and formal shape.

Mrs David Hodges
Brook Cottage, Oxon

LIGHTEN OUR DARKNESS

Gloomy areas such as a dark corner or under a yew will be brightened by a staddle-stone or similar piece there topped with a large plant in a terracotta pot. The plant won't mind the shade for a week or two and can be replaced if necessary. Trailing pelargoniums are ideal.

The Lady Bathurst
Cirencester Park, Glos

SIZE WISE

Allow at least 4¾ sq. yd/4 sq. m. when making a patio, to ensure freedom of movement behind the chairs when people are sitting round a table. And when building steps, make the rise 6 in/15 cm and the platform 18 in/45 cm.

Nigel Philips
Landscape and garden designer

BEST BEDDED

Books will tell you to lay paving slabs on 'blobs' of mortar; usually one for each corner and one in the middle of the slab. Whereas this will save on your mortar bill, it does not create a particularly strong seal and, more important, it leaves pockets where slugs, ants, snails and all manner of creepy-crawlies can breed with complete protection. It's much better to lay the slab on a level, thick bed of mortar.

Graham Clarke
Editor, Amateur Gardening

WEED-FREE PATHS

Before laying a gravel path, cover the area with heavy black plastic sheeting perforated with a few small holes for drainage. It will not show under the gravel but will smother weeds and save years of labour and gallons of weedkiller.

The Earl Kitchener of Khartoum

COVER YOUR TRACKS

Hazel coppice, small branches, or any green wood, 1½–2 in/4–6 cm in diameter, cut in 18 in/46 cm lengths and laid cross-wise over ruts or wheel tracks or any track that is liable to become a rut, will take the weight of a large car and last several years.

Mary Goldring
Freelance economist

INSTANT LICHEN

Do you find that a new garden ornament – urn, statue or whatever – looks much too clean when first installed, and thus hideously out of place? If so, spread it over with a thick coating of yoghurt (natural flavour please; you don't want old straw-berries all over the place), and a week or two later there will be a discreet covering of lichen.

John Julius Norwich
Writer and broadcaster

BALL-COCKS AND DOOR-KNOBS

Why tolerate bleak or bland timber uprights in garden trellis-work, pergolas, arbours and so forth when they can be transformed with simple plinths and finials? Garden finials can be inexpensive if one explores DIY and hardware shops looking at furniture knobs, the finials sold for staircase newels and, where a large round finial is needed, the balls of plumber's ball-cocks. They all may need painting or staining to match the surrounding trellis and to preserve them.

The Earl of Lindsay

GLASS WALLS

Bottles (wine or whisky) laid necks inwards without mortar, make an easy-to-handle, imperishable and costless foundation for dry stone retaining walls, greatly to be preferred to hard core. They make excellent retaining walls on their own with no drainage problems, but this can raise some eyebrows.

Mary Goldring
Freelance economist

LAWNS AND GRASS

COLLECTED CLIPPINGS

Try to avoid putting weedkiller on the lawn. Use lawn sand instead so that the clippings never poison the compost or mulch.

Timothy Clark
Collector of old varieties of plants

WEED AND FEED

If your lawn is patchy and full of moss, here is a cheap way to feed the grass as well as kill the moss. Mix together three parts of sulphate of ammonia with one part of sulphate of iron. Spread one large handful over each square yard of lawn and water well if the weather is dry.

Mr and Mrs A. Heley
8 Ketchmere Close, Bucks

JAM-JAR SPREADER

Use a jam jar if you don't have a lawn spreader. Punch holes in the lid and fill the jar with fertilizer or lawn sand and shake over the area.

Mrs Elizabeth Dorling
Springfield Cottage, Bucks

MIND THE GAP

Removing a plantain or any large weed can leave a hole in the lawn. Whenever weeding, take with you some earth mixed with lawn seed to make an instant repair so that the grass will germinate before the next weed does.

Mary Spiller
Horticultural consultant, Waterperry Gardens, Oxon

LOOK THE OTHER WAY

When you put weedkiller or fertilizer on the lawn, always spread it in the opposite direction to the way you look at the grass from the house. Then you won't see the bits you've missed.

Mrs Michael Todhunter
The Old Rectory, Berks

SALTS SOLUTION

To get rid of toadstools from your lawn, water with a solution of Epsom salts.

Mrs M. Dormer
Bowdown House, Berks

GRASS PANS

I always sow two or three large pans of grass seed for transplanting to bald patches in the lawn.

Miss Elizabeth Suter
Ivy House, Oxon

LYING IN THE LONG GRASS

It's a mistake to cut grass short in hot weather – it becomes very parched. Longer grass is like a protective mulch over its own roots. And if you are plagued by rabbits, consider growing the lawn longer – the vermin will linger there and not hop into your herbaceous borders.

Andrew Lawson
Garden and landscape photographer

NO MOWING

Mowing can be avoided by keeping Chinese geese – but not if there are foxes about.

A. W. A. Baker
Old Rectory Cottage, Berks

MINIATURE MOWERS

Guinea pigs are good little mowers for a small garden. Just move their run along a foot or so a day, and the grass keeps them fed.

Joe Pitt
Headmaster

WORMS AT WORK

Never worry about wormcasts on the lawn in winter. They are evidence that the time-consuming job of aerating the grass is being done for you by the worms. And rain will soon smooth the surface.

Andrew Crowden

FEATHERED FRIENDS

Weeding a camomile lawn is extremely time-consuming, but in the spring blackbirds, thrushes and rooks can help. In their search for a supper of the snails that feed there and a camomile-lined nest, they scratch out the grass – and the hardest part is done. N.B. Lawn camomile is not the sort that tastes nice in tea.

The Lady Saye and Sele
Broughton Castle, Oxon

SHORT BACK AND SIDES

For a tidy appearance, little beats well-mown grass. But if there is not time to both mow and trim the edges, priority should be given to the latter. Longer grass with cut edges looks infinitely tidier than mown grass with ragged edges.

Norman Hudson
Technical adviser, Historic Houses Association

A CLEAN CUT

If the edge of the lawn is damaged, this is the simplest way to repair it. Make a straight cut with a spade about 1 ft/0·3 m in from the edge and two incisions on either side of it so that you can lift out a square of turf. Repeat this for the length of the damage. Then turn the sods round so that a clean-cut side forms the new edge. You may need to add a little grass seed and earth to fill in the ragged part (which is now 1 ft/0·3 m from the edge) but the repair is instant.

Gordon Welburn
Head gardener, Wardington Manor, Oxon

STAY ON BOARD

Cut down the work of keeping your lawn neat by edging it with wooden boards, cut to the height of the lawn so that the mower can run over them. Cheap, simple, effective and attractive.

Mrs M. Dormer
Bowdown House, Berks

COPY THE COLLEGES

For those fastidious of lawn edges, copy Oxford colleges and order from your local metal basher strips of metal with sharp pointed pegs affixed every few feet. Push them in round the edges of your lawns, and even heavy wheelbarrows will be able to run over them with impunity.

The Hon. Mrs Tyser

A GOOD LINE-UP

In order to prevent grass growing over adjacent paving and to give a clean, well-defined line to the edge of the lawn, push a half-moon turf cutter into the crevice. This is more effective than using shears, as well as being quicker and less tedious. The lawn should be slightly above the paving to facilitate mowing.

Geoffrey Coombs
Garden adviser

STRIMMING ALONG

Using a strimmer to cut the edges of your lawn can save quite a lot of time. However, it is important to have the line very short or you will flick up all manner of stones and rubbish. This can result in broken windows, as we know to our cost. And wear a face visor.

Nicholas Charrington
Layer Marney Tower, Essex

SPEEDY TRIM

If you have a large amount of lawn edges to be trimmed, use a battery-operated Spin Trim. It quarters the time for cutting straight or curved edges and has the advantage of spreading the cuttings instead of leaving them on the path or bed. For best results, half-moon the edges first in the spring.

Mrs Phillip Trevor-Jones
Preen Manor, Shrops

BARKING MAD

How to prevent your dog from digging a moat round a hedgehog it has met on the croquet lawn: put a bucket over the prickly creature and after a while the dog will become tired of barking at a bucket. When it has gone, remove the bucket; the hedgehog will remove itself.

The Lord Feversham
Duncombe Park, N Yorks

MOW THEM DOWN

Environmentally conscious gardeners might like to sprinkle salt on to individual lawn weeds in preference to a chemical weedkiller. Follow the treatment by regular cutting with the latest recycling mower from America. This chops the grass clippings so finely that they are returned to the lawn as a powdery mulch, eliminating the disposal of mowings.

Kim Macfie
Hayter, Lawnmowers

BETTER LATE

I always try to cut the grass in bulb areas as late in the winter as possible (even January or February) so that when the small bulbs come through they are not half-hidden or fighting with too much tufty grass.

The Hon. Mrs Payne
Scotlands Farm, Berks

THE UNKINDEST CUT

To ensure that your daffodils flower year after year,

never cut the grass in which they are growing until the leaves have completely died down. In the north of England this means not a day before 1st July, sometimes 15 July in a late year. The grass may look awful (which is why many people cut too soon), but it recovers.

The Lord Ridley
Blagdon, Northumberland

OFF WITH THEIR HEADS

I use a strimmer to dead-head daffodils in grass. It requires a fairly steady hand but no harm seems to come to the daffodils if you can leave at least 6 in/15 cm of foliage.

Mrs J. Wilkerson
Admington Hall, Warks

… I use a hazel switch for dead-heading daffodils.

The Lady Fanshawe

DARLING DAISY

Perhaps we should learn to love the daisies in the lawn. When I take Americans round gardens they exclaim over 'the dear little daisies' and ask how we manage to grow them so prettily in the grass. They are amazed when I explain that our one ambition is to get rid of them. It would certainly be much easier to let them stay – and they *are* pretty.

Mrs J. Baker
NGS Hon.County Organizer, Oxon

LAWN SNOBS

In spring my garden is blue with ceanothus, forget-me-nots and bluebells; in early summer it becomes multi-coloured with red, yellow and white roses. But fundamentally it is a green garden – a matter of leaves and lawn. There are some people – I regard them as lawn snobs – who insist on the purest unmixed grass for their lawn. Their punishment is to be continually marching up and down with mowers. I also like a green effect, but achieved with a variety of mosses, dandelion leaves, clover, self-heal and what other people call weeds. I seldom have to patrol like a soldier on guard duty. My lawn, much enriched through its variety, looks after itself.

Michael Holroyd
Author

POOLS AND PONDS

A TOUGH START

Nothing is more boring than a Labrador or water spaniel that *will* jump into a swimming-pool – especially if there are people in it. We took a firm line with our new puppy and threw him into the deep end when he was very young. It gave him such a fright that although he swims happily in open water he never ventures into the pool.

William Davies
Artist

BLACK AND BLUE

Paint a swimming pool dark blue or black – it will look far more natural than the inevitable brilliant turquoise, which looks vulgar even in the Caribbean.

David Hicks
Interior decorator and garden designer

BREAKING THE RULES

If you decide on a pond for your garden, resign yourself to an algae-ridden swamp. At least then you won't be disappointed. I read all the literature before starting on mine. Dutifully I followed the advice on dimensions, volume, siting, preparation, planting and stocking, envisaging as I laboured a lily-laden oasis with fish darting and plunging into limpid waters. It took two weeks from filling the pond to acquire the khaki hue that so repels visitors. In summer, the fish deign to appear, briefly, at feeding time, before disappearing for a bit more horseplay in the impenetrable depths that start two inches below the surface. I know of two garden ponds which stay crystal clear the year round affording vistas of gambolling goldfish. Both were built without so much as a glance at a book and both defy all the rules of pond construction.

Peter Rogers
Editor, Grower

THE LAST STRAW

It seems too simple to be effective but barley straw – it *must* be barley – will keep water free from weed. About a quarter of a bale in an average garden pond will do the trick.

Anthony Archer-Wills
Pond and water-garden specialist

CRYSTAL POOLS

To keep garden pools crystal clear add a bag of live daphne (sold in pet shops as fish food) and *don't* keep fish.

Stella Caws
Landscape and garden designer

THINK BIG

We have a weed-cutting boat which, as you can imagine, is a very expensive item, but it means that one man can cut 8 acres of weeds in less than two days. Then with a small tractor on the bank and the weed-cutting boat in the middle, we drag the weeds round the lake with a boom made of logs tied together with nylon rope. The boom is about 50 yd/45 m long. It takes about a day to drag the weeds into a corner of the lake and they are then removed by a JCB which loads them onto tractors and trailers. The first cut takes place in May or June and usually fills about sixty trailers. We carry out about two or three subsequent cuts and probably remove 120 loads of dreadful smelling muck. For the final cut in August we leave the weed in one corner of the lake and place an automatic duck-feeder near it so that the duck feed is sprayed out over the weed and the ducks then push it all to the bottom of the lake. We have developed this system over many years and it is the cheapest and most efficient way I know of. It requires only two men and about fifteen days' work.

Sir Francis Dashwood
West Wycombe Park, Bucks

FROZEN FISH

If you worry about the goldfish in your ornamental pond suffering in icy weather, float a large ball or corked bottle on the surface. If it ices over you can easily make a breathing hole by removing the floaters. It is bad for the fish to break the ice by hammering it – the blows can stun them.

Marco Pierre White
Restaurateur

ARUM LILIES

If you have a shallow garden pool, or a pond with shallow edges, nothing is prettier on a sunny day than arum lilies reflected in the water. I plant mine in 12 in/30 cm pots and sink them so that water covers the edges and only the stems and leaves are visible. Stand them on a couple of bricks if you need a firmer base. The roots won't freeze under water and the plants obligingly reappear the next spring. Alternatively they can be rescued in the autumn and kept in a cool place. This way you get earlier flowering.

Mrs John Hawksworth

SWAG BAG

I find expensive water lilies difficult to establish. They often leave without saying goodbye. Instead of planting them in those plastic baskets, create a 'swag bag' by laying wire netting on the ground, covering it with a layer of newspaper and a good mound of soil enclosing the lily. Draw up the wire netting and garrotte lightly round the plant's neck with wire. The roots will establish themselves through the netting without further repotting.

Lady Edmonstone
Duntreath Castle, by Glasgow

WATER TIGHT

It is always necessary to line aquatic containers in order to prevent the soil washing away into the water of the pool. Tights can easily be stretched over the container to keep the soil in place and won't show in the water. Simply cut a small hole to plant through.

Adam Pasco
Editor, BBC Gardener's World

PURPLE DEEPS

A new pond lined with concrete or brick usually needs to be painted with a pond seal to prevent lime scale and furred-up pipes. This can be quite expensive but can be rendered unnecessary by sprinkling potassium permanganate, which will neutralize the lime, into the water as soon as the pond is finished. Leave it for a couple of days – the water will turn purple – drain it, refill and all will be well.

James Montagu
Pond and water-garden specialist

PERFECT PLEASURES

As a child I derived intense pleasure from a small pond in a sink in our suburban back garden in Sheffield. A pond of my own was my dream for years, and now I have one, built for me by my gardener son Joe in a kiln under our house in West Somerset. It is circular and rejoices in eight-eenth-century brickwork dripping with ferns at the back and 1991 stonework round the edges. One of the great joys of a water garden, I have discovered, is that if it is well balanced it looks after itself, so it is ideal for those like myself who are busy, lazy and often abroad. It is stocked with three shy goldfish, two very shy golden orfe and three invisible green tench, and a lot of interesting plants. It really requires very little attention, though I can sit by it for hours.

Margaret Drabble
Author

THE WONDERS OF WEEDING

POSITION IS EVERYTHING
A weed is a good plant in the wrong place.

Mrs John Lowther
Guilsborough Court, Northants

KNOW THE ENEMY
Weeds are always with us and it is wise to get to know them in all their stages but particularly when they are small so that one can literally nip them in the bud. So often they cleverly grow next to a good plant with a very similar leaf and it is quite difficult to distinguish bad from good.

Miss R. Hartas Jackson
Maypole Cottage, Berks

THE PLEASURES OF WEEDING
Weeding is one of the most enjoyable of gardening occupations. In bringing your eyes close to the ground (and you should never be ashamed of

getting down on your hands and knees) you'll see and take note of so many interesting things which you would otherwise miss. The small animals you turn up with your trowel, for instance. Get to know your friends (generally the ones like centipedes which move fast) and which are eating your plants (which remain relatively inactive or slow-moving). Learn to identify all the common weeds, so that when something uncommon has self-sown from a valued plant, you won't destroy it.

Christopher Lloyd
Gardening correspondent, Country Life

TAKE A TRUG

A very old gardener in Bath told me never to walk round the garden without a trug or basket. It is only too easy to pull out a piece of ground elder or couch grass and, having nowhere to put it, drop it, intending to dispose of it later. But one inevitably forgets and the resulting growth makes even more work in the end.

Mrs Peter Toynbee
NGS Hon. County Oganizer, Bucks

TESTING

Question: When should you pull out a weed?
Answer: Whenever you see it. Most people don't.

Mrs John Lowther
Guilsborough Court, Northants

TWEAKED

I use eye-brow tweezers for weeding amongst fragile potted plants and seedlings.

Miss Elizabeth Suter
Ivy House, Oxon

GETTING RID OF GROUND ELDER

To get rid of ground elder – even the Romans were plagued with it in England – and any other difficult perennial weeds, spray the area thoroughly with a glyphosate herbicide on a dry day when there is no likelihood of rain for six hours. Make sure you wet all the weed foliage but do not spray the leaves of any garden plants. Then keep a sharp watch on the area and, at the first sight of any regeneration, spray again, this time holding the sprayer close to the weed leaves, with a piece of cardboard or wood in the free hand to protect neighbouring plants from drift. Repeat as necessary and do not allow any fragment of weed to reappear. Two or three such treatments are likely to destroy it completely.

Arthur Hellyer
Horticultural journalist and photographer

SMOTHERED

On moving house I found myself with a garden where the predominant plant was ground elder – so much everywhere that some reasonably inexpensive means were required to be rid of it. So we cut it down and then covered it with a thick layer of mown grass, keeping this up all summer, never allowing even one leaf of the weed to see the light of day. At the end of the year it was nearly eliminated, and by the following year completely. This can be done round shrubs and over bulbs without harming them – in fact, aconites love the mulch.

The Countess Cathcart

LEAF THE WEEDS

We are on our fourth garden and in each one we

112

have had mature trees. Their leaves were never burned: they were 'placed', I mean placed, held between two hands, on every shrub bed, 4–6 in/10–15 cm thick. They were not first rotted. Any goodness in them went first into the soil and worms would also take them down. Placed on damp beds they kept the beds moistened and *would not allow* weeds to grow – the odd ones perhaps, but these could easily be pulled out. Leaves are good because they make humus and are a better mulch than peat which has no goodness or food value.

Catherine Cookson
Author

MOW IT OUT

If your herbaceous border is thick with bindweed, turf it over completely in the autumn and mow it out over the next few years. Glamorous shrubs can replace the herbaceous plants, leaving space for mowing in between, and any surviving bindweed can be untwined and killed.

Mrs D. Royle
Home Farm, Oxon

NO COME BACK

Convolvulus is a wretched nuisance, but I can now get rid of it in one operation. Wait until May or June when there is quite a lot of leaf and stem. Carefully and patiently unwind it all and lay it in a heap on the ground – this gives quite the same sort of satisfaction as solving a crossword. Now saturate the unfortunate plant with Tumbleweed. It won't make a comeback.

Orlando Murrin
Deputy editor, Living

HAND IN GLOVE

For dealing with bindweed: put an old woollen glove over a rubber glove and, armed with a wide-mouthed jar of mixed Roundup, you have an ever-ready secret weapon. Soak the glove in the jar and run it along the length of the bindweed. It helps to have a very big woollen glove that you can slip on easily.

Lady Anne Rasch
Heale Gardens, Wilts

... We use this method but we add flour to make a glutinous mixture, stroking the mess on to the weeds, leaving a floury residue so that we can see which we have poisoned.

Mrs S. Hoskins
Ashley Manor, Glos

... When bindweed is growing enthusiastically among other plants it is difficult to dab it with Tumbleweed without murdering the good guys. Put some stakes in amongst it and when it has ramped up them it will be easy to paint it or grasp it with a weedkiller glove.

Nicholas Bell
Practicality Brown, garden contractor

A DAB HAND

Save an old roll-on deodorant bottle and fill it with weedkiller, so that as you walk round the garden you can dab here and there, killing weeds as they catch your eye. But be sure to label it well so that it doesn't find its way back to the bathroom shelf.

Robin Lane Fox
Gardening author and journalist

MAGIC CARPET

I don't have as much time to dig and look after my allotment as I would like, and in the winter when I have harvested the crops, such as they are, the weeds grow. I have found a useful way to prevent this. I simply find a piece of old carpet and lay it over the ground. It keeps the weeds down wonderfully and helps to compost those caught underneath. Such a practice also helps in that old carpet can be difficult to get rid of and this is a useful purpose for it. Aesthetically it is perhaps not the most beautiful method but then allotments in the middle of winter rarely are beautiful, and it is very effective.

Tony Baldry MP

MIND YOUR EYE

Before you start hand weeding a mixed border, place empty cartridge cases on the top of stakes or canes which surround clumps of stocks, lupins, Michaelmas daisies etc. This can prevent a very nasty accident to the eyes or face.

Sadie Watts

MINERAL WEEDERS

Salt and nitrogen are as good as most weedkillers. Salt thrown on dew-covered leaves of nettles in the morning will kill them by nightfall. Small concentrated applications of nitrogen will burn out most weeds and the surrounding plants will grow better for the fertilizer.

Timothy Clark
Collector of old varieties of plants

115

A PINCH OF SALT

One of the safest ways to kill a weed such as a dandelion or plantain is to put a good pinch of salt right into the middle. The weed will die and the plants round will be unharmed, as is not always the case with sprayed weedkiller.

Mrs Mary Tolley

BRAMBLING

There is nothing more satisfying than removing brambles from rhododendrons. Place a sturdy, narrow, four-pronged fork under the bramble root, slip a log behind the fork and, using this as a fulcrum, ease the roots out. A short sermon, roast beef and an afternoon brambling is Sunday at its best!

The Earl of Shelburne
Bowood House, Wilts

STRIMMED

The best weed suppression I know is the regular use of a strimmer. Soon there will be grass where there have been nettles and brambles – and I am talking from experience in our woodland garden.

Mrs B. S. Barlow
Stancombe Park, Glos

LET SLEEPING SEEDS LIE

Annual weed seeds germinate only if they are very near the surface. Removing them with a draw-hoe disturbs the soil too much, bringing the dormant seeds nearer to the top. It's better to use a push-pull hoe or a swoe which just skims the weeds off the surface leaving the seeds lower down undisturbed where they will remain dormant.

David Hollinrake
Horticultural therapist

HOE, HOE

If you hoe when you don't need to hoe, you *never* need to hoe.

A. Aslett
1 The Green, Cheddington, Beds

SMOTHERED

When couch grass is growing into other plants, it is difficult, if not impossible, to dig it out without damaging the neighbours; sow tomato seeds amongst it in the spring. In the summer you have to put up with the strange sight of tomatoes growing in unlikely places, but in the autumn the tomatoes die off and so does the couch grass.

H H Judge James Fox-Andrews

SPRAY AWAY

For many years we have been looking for a solution to the problem of Japanese knotweed. We tried everything in the book to diminish its enthusiasm for spreading all over the Wild Garden. We have at last found the killer: it is a farm spray by the name of Grazon 90. In the same breath our solution to the nettle problem is Garlon 2. The best time to spray is when the nettles are still young in late April/early May. The effect can last for several years.

Commander L. M. M. Saunders Watson
Rockingham Castle, Leics

CROWDED OUT

The best way for the weekend gardener to keep weeds down is to keep planting. The more you plant the more difficult it is for the weeds to grow and you will get much more satisfaction from the results.

Lady Olga Maitland MP

FUNGUS FUGIT

An emulsion of 1 pt/600 ml creosote to 2 gal/9 l water (stirred not shaken) is an inexpensive and effective way of dealing with honey fungus. Apply to the soil avoiding leaves, and be prepared for a temporary browning of the grass.

Paul Miles
Garden designer

COURT SPRAY

To kill moss on a tennis court, spray it with one part Jeyes Fluid to four parts water.

Rosemary, Marchioness of Northampton

FRAUD AND ILLUSION

I firmly believe that if you mow your lawn and cut your edges and tidy the first 6 in/15 cm of the borders, nobody, but nobody notices the bindweed and nettles growing up with the taller plants at the back. I feel this is a very useful hint for the home gardener.

Michael Upward
Secretary, The Alpine Garden Society

PRETTY WEEDY

I have learnt, with diligence and application, to love weeds. Life is too short to despair for long at an untidy flower-bed; and my husband (an artist) has taught me to see the beauty in a dandelion – and the joy to be had from a lawn speckled with daisies and speedwell.

Gabrielle Drake
Actress

PLAGUES AND PESTS

PREVENTION IS BETTER THAN CURE

Begin each gardening year by spraying susceptible shrubs, soft fruit bushes and perennials on a regular basis with a suitable insecticide and fungicide *before* the bugs strike.

Mrs J. Nicholson
Bucksbridge House, Bucks

UP THE SPOUT

If you have a pot plant with a heavy infestation of white-fly, try this. Put the plant on the floor, taking care not to disturb the flies. Get out the vacuum cleaner, put it on to full suck with no nozzle on the tube, and hold it over the plant. Rattle the plant, the flies will swarm into the air ... the sheer delight of watching the little pests being sucked into oblivion is most rewarding. More advanced students may like to try this in the garden with an exterior lead.

Patrick Braddell
Treasurer, Simon Weatherby Garden Trust,
Katharine House Hospice

FLIES AWAY

Plant french marigolds in the soil border of the greenhouse among your tomato plants. They will keep white-fly at bay – or, at least, they do for me.

Alan Titchmarsh
Gardening writer and broadcaster

... I plant basil in my greenhouse to deter white-fly.

Mrs Andrea Bates

... Use the encorsa wasp (you can buy the eggs in sachets at a garden centre, and they will hatch in a greenhouse) to eat white-fly in greenhouses – it won't harm you and will do far less damage than chemicals.

Anthea Gibson
Garden designer, Westwell Manor, Glos

FLY SPRAY

As a spray for roses, a teaspoonful of Jeyes Fluid and a tablespoon of Maincrop (or similar), added to 2 gal/9 l water in a watering can, will get rid of all green- and white-fly.

Mrs Rosalind Squire
Tibby's Cottage, Bucks

... Boil up scraps of soap – three teaspoonfuls to 1 gal/4·5 l of water – and use the resultant liquid as a spray against greenfly, white-fly, ants etc. Sometimes the fragrance in expensive ones stops them sticking to the target. A few squirts of Fairy Liquid overcomes this.

A. E. H. Heber Percy
Hodnet Hall, Shrops

SMOKE OUT

Here's one way to rid your indoor plants of aphids. Give a dinner party once a week and send all post-prandial puffers into the conservatory. Your smokers will for once feel environmentally valuable, you will be a most popular hostess amongst tycoons and teenagers and, best of all, your conservatory will be bug-free.

Sue Prideaux
Garden designer

FAG ENDS

Should your roses suffer from an infestation of aphids (of any colour), become a cigarette-butt collector. When you have filled a large saucepan – encourage heavy smokers – add some water and boil them for half an hour. Strain, and spray the resultant revolting liquid on the affected plants.

The Lord Sackville
Knole, Kent

LOOK, NO CHEMICALS

If your roses are plagued with black spot and if you prefer not to use chemicals, you will control it quite successfully if you prune in November and remove any leaves remaining on the bushes. In very cold areas remove as much of the top growth as possible and all the leaves in autumn, then give them a final trim in March. After about two seasons, black spot infection will be at an acceptable level.

Daphne Ledward
Gardening adviser and broadcaster

MULCH AGAIN

Mulching your rose beds, especially with well-rotted lawn clippings in the spring, prior to leaf emergence, helps to prevent black spot.

Mrs Thomas Egerton
Heads Farm, Berks

HERBAL CURES

Parsley grown in or near a rose border will help to prevent black spot.

Margaret Laborde

… Chives used as an edging for rose beds are said to keep away various rose diseases such as black spot. My success with this has not been 100 per cent, but the effect is pretty and the results useful in the kitchen.

A.du Gard Pasley
Landscape architect

MIX IT

Avoid monocultures. Enjoy as wide a range of different kinds of plants as the site allows. Monoculture, for instance a mania for growing roses, leads to tunnel vision; also a moving-in of all the pests which your chosen favourite is subject to. The more you grow of one thing the easier it becomes for its pests and parasites to find it out and wreak devastation. If you mix your ingredients they'll all be happy. But your eye must be vigilant to ensure fair play.

Christopher Lloyd
Gardening correspondent, Country Life

PEPPERMINT PROTECTION

Grow a patch of pennyroyal in cool moist ground. Rub a fresh sprig of this peppermint-scented herb across the path of any ant you spot in the house – the insects hate it and will go elsewhere. It will also repel cat fleas, so sprinkle a few sprigs in the cat's basket.

Lesley Bremness
Herb grower and garden designer

SLUGS

Half scooped-out grapefruit or orange skins left lying face down in strategic parts of the garden will attract slugs and snails at night. In the morning all you have to do is gather the pests up and dispose of them.

HM Queen Elizabeth The Queen Mother

… Horsehair, coarsely twisted and put round a plant will protect it from slugs who do not like the prickly ends of the hair.

Elizabeth Jane Howard
Author

… Half fill a bowl with second-class beer. Put it on your lawn or flower-bed, if possible making a depression in the ground so that the rim of the bowl is at ground level. The slugs will smell the beer, approach, drink, fall into the bowl and die a happy death.

This is not a joke.

Kingsley Amis
Author

… Cover all hosta plants before they come up (if

124

you know where they are) with very fine gravel. Slugs loath gritty surfaces and will leave them strictly alone.

Mrs Moran Caplat

SUBSTITUTE SPIRES

If you would dearly love to grow delphiniums but never succeed because of slugs and snails, grow *Aconitum napellus* instead. These are so poisonous that the pests will leave them alone and you will have beautiful 5 ft/1·5 m tall spires at the back of your border at last.

Jill Fenwick
Garden designer and illustrator

PERFUMED PESTICIDE

A few granules of Paradichlorobenzene, sold by the chemist as moth crystals, sprinkled into the bottom of containers when potting house plants will eliminate most soil pests. They have the additional advantage that as they evaporate over a period of several days they release a perfume more pleasant than the majority of conventional pesticides.

Bill Keen
Hon. Editor, British Cactus and Succulent Journal

STAMP 'EM OUT

My great-aunt would stick dry, hollow stems of hemlock into the flower-beds. Any earwigs within crawling distance would obligingly creep in at night. In the morning my aunt would tap them out on to the flagstones and stamp on them.

Michael Inchbald
Architectural and interior designer

... An upturned flower-pot filled with straw on a stick is a humane way to trap earwigs and guaranteed not to harm them.

Kate Morley
Editor, The Complete Florist

DOWN FLEW THE BLACKBIRD

A good lady writing to a gardening magazine in 1982 had her own way of dealing with pests. She said, 'Our earwig traps are not at all unsightly. We crush sheets of newspaper into fairly tight balls, hide them among the dahlia foliage, and overnight the insects crawl into the screwed-up paper. Then in the morning after breakfast, we go into the garden, call to the blackird, "Earwig, Blackie," and he flies down to quickly devour the earwigs that scurry out as we shake the ball.'

Hannah Gordon
Actress

MOTH-EATEN

Codling-moth larvae are the number-one apple and pear pests. They have eight pairs of legs and burrow into the fruit through the eye and feed near the core, only to be discovered when you take a bite. The easiest method of control in a garden is to hang pheromone traps (obtainable from Steele and Brodie Ltd, telephone 0794 388 698) among your trees between mid-May and early September. A sex attractant in the trap lures the male moth on to the sticky surface from which he cannot escape to breed. In this way you can ensure fewer fertilized eggs and maggots, without also harming more beneficial insects.

Winter moth caterpillars have legs only at the front and back ends, looping their bodies when moving. They hatch out from late April and nibble young leaves, buds and blossom of apple trees before dropping to the ground in June to pupate. The best antidote is to apply grease bands round the stem of each tree in late September; these trap the wingless female moths as they climb up in autumn to lay their eggs.

Bonham Bazeley
Fruit tree specialist

TAKE TO THE BOTTLE

We have a lot of trouble with wasps when lunching by the pool or barbecue. We find they can't resist cider, of which we leave an inch or so in old tonic bottles (laid on their sides). They crawl in, get drunk and drown. It is such a success that we have to keep on replacing the bottles.

HRH Princess Michael of Kent

BIRD SCARER

Here's a way to protect newly sown seeds. Take a large clean potato and stick pheasant feathers into it so that it resembles a hovering bird. Thread a string through it and suspend it from a stick over the seed bed. It will keep birds away because they will think it is a hawk or kestrel.

Mrs John Puxley
Welford Park, Berks

NO BAIT FOR BIRDS

No one wants to kill birds, so always put mouse traps or poison baits in lengths of drainpipe – mice will always sneak along them but birds never will.

Lord Montagu of Beaulieu
Palace House, Hants

OWL-WISE

To prevent swallows from nesting in a doorless garage – and one's car from being covered in bird droppings – hang something that resembles an owl. Swallows hate owls.

Rosemary, Marchioness of Northampton

POTTY-TRAINED

I love my two cats very much but do not appreciate the way they perceive my small garden as one big litter tray. I have finally trained them to use the back patch of spare earth by using a mulch of cocoa shells on every other inch of my garden. Maybe it's the smell of chocolate that puts them off.

Pattie Barron
Gardening editor, Evening Standard

PUSS OFF

Cats' favourite thing is to roll about on newly planted seed beds. Stick small bushy twigs in the ground, dotted about. That'll stop them.

Capt J. Hope

KEEP OUT

To discourage cats from coming into the garden,

put large lemonade bottles full of water in places where they like to go. This will keep them away – I don't know why.

Ray Gravel
Presenter, Streetlife, *BBC Wales*

PINK PROTECTION
Epsom salts sprinkled round dianthus will keep rabbits away.

Judith Bannister
Head gardener, Kiftsgate Court, Glos

NIBBLE-PROOF
Six plants that I would suggest in a border which our friend Mrs Rabbit does not seem to like but which will provide colour over many months: *Astilbe*, the Himalayan blue poppy *Meconopsis barteyii*, *Sedum* 'Autumn Joy', *Geranium macrorrhizum* 'Walter Ingwersen', willow gentian and finally the thorniest moss or species roses whose stems prove too much for even the bravest nibbler, a modern equivalent being the magnificent 'Cerise Bouquet'.

Mrs Bryce McCosh
Dalemain, Cumbria

RODENT PROOFING
Soak all autumn-planted spring-flowering bulbs, in particular the smaller ones such as crocuses and tulips, in a solution of a tablespoon of paraffin to 1 pt/600 ml water for thirty minutes. This will prevent rodents such as squirrels, rabbits, rats etc. from digging them up and eating them.

Brian Davis
Garden consultant and lecturer

MEMORIES

Old horseshoes scattered on the surface of freshly planted ground keeps rabbits away – apparently the pests have a folk memory of gin traps.

Kit Hall
Ashford Manor, Shrops

ON GUARD

We weekend gardeners fight an almost losing battle against rabbits who ravage our gardens. They dig under walls and tear through fencing. I make generous use of plastic tree-guards which may be ugly but are definitely useful. If the plant is small, cut the tree-guard in half, to make sure the plant has sufficient light.

Lady Olga Maitland MP

HAPPY BIRTHDAY

My neighbour, the widow of the Vicar of Loweswater, had trouble with moles. She got rid of them by putting a musical birthday card down their hole. They never came back, once they'd heard 'Happy Birthday' for the 300th time.

Hunter Davies
Author and broadcaster

CAMPHORATED

I was infested with moles until I managed to put moth balls into their runs. My neighbour is still troubled by them but they haven't come into my garden since.

Frank Morgan
Retired diplomat

WHIRL AWAY

Place a child's windmill into the molehill. The vibrations as it whirls around will scare the moles away – and make your garden look animated.

Mrs Roy Petrie

MOLE-DOG

If you want to get rid of moles, try to become the owner of a mole-catching dog. My Labrador caught a hundred in 1991.

HRH Princess Alice Duchess of Gloucester

RHUBARB, RHUBARB

When you see a molehill in the garden, stuff a stick of rhubarb into the hole. Moles loathe rhubarb and will depart. I've used this method with great effect. I hope it wasn't coincidental.

Lady Owen
Bickerstaff Farm, Warks

DEPARTED

We live in a part of the country where the woods give protection to a species of small but very predatory deer. They descend every night into the valley. Walls and fences present little obstacle to them and they constantly raid gardens where they particularly fancy young rose shoots. To deter their activities, soak rags in Renardine, available at most hardware stores. We set the rags on sticks to form an inconspicuous barrier. Apparently the smell is deeply offensive to deer. Obviously, the rags have to be redipped after heavy rain.

The Duchess of Norfolk
Arundel Castle, Sussex

... Our deer defence method is to make small bags from old tights and fill them with human hair (not shampooed). We attach these loosely to stakes or bamboo canes so that they will blow in the wind, and surround the area to be protected with the bags at 6–8 ft/1·8–2·4 m intervals. We renew the hair frequently. It is no good if it is clean.

Anne, Duchess of Rutland

... We protect plants, shrubs, hedges etc. from browsing deer by soaking pieces of string or binder twine in creosote and laying or tying them in vulnerable parts. The deer *will* stay away. Shepherds in Scotland put a finger-tip dab of creosote on newly born lambs' necks to protect them from foxes.

The Duke of Buccleuch
Boughton House, Northants

NUMBER ONE DEFENCE

If your garden suffers from marauding badgers, give a dinner party and invite as many men as possible. Give them lots of wine and while the ladies retire upstairs, turn them out into the garden. Suitably directed they can 'mark your territory' around the boundaries where the badgers enter. This will unfailingly deter them as they will not trespass into another's territory. After heavy rain you have a lovely excuse for another party.

Annabel Allhusen
Garden designer

PROPAGATING AND
POTTING ON

KEEP MOVING

In the greenhouse, frequent spacing and grading of plants on the bench ensures even growth and development of full potential. It is preferable to grow fewer plants and have fine specimens, than to have many of poor quality.

John Watkins
Glasshouse supervisor, Royal Horticultural Society Gardens, Wisley

LITTLE AND OFTEN

When trying to root difficult cuttings, take two or three cuttings each month, instead of a lot all at one go.

Barry Boden
Gardener, Upton House, Warks

HOLE IN ONE

How did we ever manage without yoghurt pots for seedlings? It is just a shame that they don't come with ready-made drainage holes! However, I have found that the simplest way to pierce them is to heat a skewer or metal knitting needle over a gas or candle flame and push it through their bottoms.

Mrs R. A. Aldridge
Weir Lodge, Bucks

ROOTS REVEALED

The rectangular plastic containers in which peaches and nectarines are sold are ideal for cuttings. The bottom is clear so that one can easily see when the roots have formed.

Denis Patrick
Holly House, Bucks

COMPARTMENTS

When sowing seeds of flowers or vegetables, I always use one of those plastic seed-tray liners with small compartments which one can buy from garden centres for a few pence. Sow only two or three seeds in each compartment. This saves seed and avoids the boring job of pricking-out – and even more important, means that the young plants can be potted on or planted out without root disturbance so that they grow far quicker. Tray and liners can be re-used again and again if handled carefully.

John Landell Mills
Chairman, Kelways Nurseries

GOOD LITTLE SEED TRAYS

Wash out empty margarine tubs, make drainage

holes in the bottom, fill with seed compost and you have good little seed trays.

Glenda Jackson MP

IN TRAYS

Beg used polystyrene pot trays from a florist who sells large quantities of pot plants. For a gardener who grows many plants in pots in the greenhouse they are invaluable, enabling him to keep varieties and colours together and saving time moving plants within, and out of, the greenhouse or cold-frame to the planting area. These trays hold fifteen and eighteen pots. They also prevent plants from getting knocked over.

Albert Reed
Head gardener, Swyncombe House, Oxon

POTTING UP

Whenever I'm potting up at Kiftsgate I wish the work bench were 3¼ ft/1 m high which would be just the right height to prevent backache and fatigue.

Lady Hobson

… If you're pricking out at a table, raise the level of the seed tray by standing it on a large upturned pot.

Mrs J. A. K. Leslie
Kincora, Bucks

AT THE READY

Always have a tray of potting compost (half peat, half sharpsand) handy, so that when you need to plant cuttings in a hurry the tray is ready and waiting – all you need to do is pop them in.

Mrs John Boughey
NGS Hon. County Organizer, Northants

TRAVEL BAG

Like every enthusiastic plantswoman, I collect cuttings wherever I go. I find the best way to keep them until I get home is in a plastic bag. The trick is to blow the bag up like a balloon and fasten it securely so that the cuttings are kept in their own micro-climate. Don't add water; it seems to damp them off. I brought rose cuttings safely home from India in this way and even at the end of the journey, two weeks later, they were fresh and well.

Mrs D.H. Binny
Kiftsgate, Glos

ROOTING FOR SUCCESS

Use a white polythene bag to enclose all soft-shoot cuttings rooted in pots of damp peat and soft sand. They can then be stood on a warm sunny window-sill – the white polythene allows sufficient light for growth but not so much that it scorches. A small stick in the pot to keep the polythene off the leaves reduces the chance of soft rot.

Peter Seabrook
Gardening writer and television presenter

IT'S IN THE BAG

Instead of putting polythene bags *over* pots of cuttings, put the pot *in* the bag, blow air into it and do it up with a twisty tie. This method keeps the bag from touching the foliage and condensation is easily corrected by just opening the top. To prevent sun-scorching use opaque polythene.

Ann Watson
Horticultural lecturer, South Glamorgan Institute

LOOK, NO GREENHOUSE

To bring plants on if you haven't got a greenhouse: fill a lot of sacks with grass cuttings and damp them down well. Put boxes of plants in a cold-frame and surround them top and sides with these filled sacks. They will generate enough heat to keep the plants warm and healthy during the winter and bring them on for planting out in the spring when you remove the sacks.

Frank Hands

LEARN FROM EXPERIENCE

The essence of good growing lies in timing. I find that keeping a propagation book of sowing and cuttings times makes a valuable reference, especially if failures as well as successes are recorded.

John Watson
Retired plantsman

ONE AT A TIME

I use eyebrow tweezers to sow seeds at the correct distance in either boxes or open ground; then I find I don't have to thin out and I don't waste any seeds.

Denis Patrick
Holly House, Bucks

SORBUS SEEDS

The seeds of mountain ash and whitebeam normally take two years to germinate. Sometimes they can be persuaded to start in the first spring by first removing all the pulp from the pod, washing and drying the seeds, putting them in the deep freeze for a month and then sowing in the spring.

The Lord Ridley
Blagdon, Northumberland

SEED TIMING

Write the year of purchase on unfinished seed packets before you fold them over to put them away in a dry drawer. Sow your new lettuce seed in spring, for it gets away faster than old, which serves for summer.

Mrs P. Bradly
Whiteknights, Berks

PARSLEY PROBLEMS

One of the most difficult herbs to grow is parsley, whose problems are based in the very hard casing of the seed. Put the seeds in an old cup and pour very hot water into it. Then mix them with some dry sand, which will make them go further, and sow them in well composted or manured ground. Sow twice, once in the spring and again in the summer.

Jack Percival
Head gardener, Quoitings, Bucks

EASTER TASK

Always plant parsley on Good Friday.

Olive French

RECYCLED ROLLS

Sow sweet peas and parsley, which have long tap roots, in the centre of toilet rolls. They can then be planted out at the appropriate time, in the cardboard, without disturbing the seedlings.

Mrs J. S. Rivers
Homeland, Oxon

NEWSPAPER POTS

I make individual tubes out of newspaper for sweet-pea seeds. A job for long winter evenings; it is well worth the trouble because you just pop the seedlings, in their tubes, straight into the prepared bed without disturbing their roots.

Elizabeth Suter
Ivy House, Oxon

SPEEDY SEEDS

Here's a good way to germinate seeds quickly. It works best with large ones such as sweet peas, onions, cucumbers etc. Place blotting paper in the bottom of an airtight ice-cream carton and soak it well. Drain off the water, lay the seeds on the wet paper and close the lid tightly. Put the container in a warm position and check the seeds every twenty-four hours. When they show signs of life pick them out individually and plant in pots.

Albert Reed
Head gardener, Swyncombe House, Oxon

PATIENCE

For years I have sown seed of hybrid alstroemeria with great care but no success. I put it in the airing cupboard, put it in the freezer – all the tricks kind friends told me. As a final gesture three years ago I scattered some seed in the border and this year I am at last rewarded by a good show of shoots. Evidently I should have been more patient.

Mrs Micky Rooney

TOPS

Cut off the bottom of a round, transparent plastic bottle. Remove the screw top to allow for ventilation. Place on a pot of cuttings or seedlings for a cheap propagator.

Valerie Day
Horticultural lecturer and consultant

SURPRISES

When I lose patience with a tray of seeds that won't come up, I tip the compost into a particular corner of the greenhouse. I keep an eye on it and am often surprised by what changes its mind and pops up – and it's such fun guessing what on earth it's going to turn into.

Orlando Murrin
Deputy editor, Living

DULL DAY'S WORK

Harvest poppy seeds on a dull damp day. Collected in very hot summer weather, they germinate very poorly, if at all.

Miriam Rothschild
Wild flower specialist

SAFE SEEDLINGS

With tiny seedlings such as lobelia, it is best to move them in small clumps rather than try to separate them. Begonia seedlings should be allowed to develop leaves almost the size of a penny piece before they are moved – otherwise the roots are too weak to sustain the plants. In all cases shade newly planted seedlings from bright sunlight with a single sheet of newspaper for a week until fresh growth shows they are firmly established.

Max Davidson
Assistant editor, Sunday Express

FLOW CONTROL

When watering a drill for seeds put a cork with a V-shaped slot cut down the length of it into the spout of the watering-can. This will reduce the flow most satisfactorily.

Jessica Otley

CLOCHES

I slice round the big plastic containers that spring and mineral water comes in these days and the two halves make very useful cloches which fit 7 in/17·5 cm pots. Seedlings grow very nicely protected by these.

Penny Kitchen
Editor, Home and Country

IN THE GREEN

If you want to give away bulbs of snowdrops or aconites from your garden, dig them up as soon as the flowers are over but the leaves still green. They should be split and planted in their new situation as soon as possible.

Catherine Jewison

SHAKY START

Increase aconites by taking the brown seed heads and shaking them directly into grass, preferably under trees.

Mrs G. E. Davey-Turner
The Manor House, Northants

EARLY SPLIT

It is possible to split daffodil bulbs if you dig them up when the buds are just formed. The goodness will have gone out of the bulb and into the shoots so that separating the bulbs and replanting them will do no damage.

The Rt Hon John Biffen MP

MULTIPLICATION BY DIVISION

Penstemon 'Evelyn' is a wonderful plant for dividing into lots of others. It can literally be persuaded to fall apart.

Annabel Allhusen
Garden designer

POT TO POT

When repotting plants, place the plant to be repotted in its pot within the new, empty, larger one. Fill up the space between the two with compost; firm the compost and carefully remove the inner pot. Decant the plant and pop it into its new, perfectly fitting home.

John Course
Gardening correspondent, The Guardian

EASY CUTTINGS

Cardamine pratensis (lady's smock or cuckoo flower) barely sets any seed: the pods are usually empty. However, this plant can be propagated very easily from almost any part of the stalk and the roots.

Miriam Rothschild
Wild flower specialist

DO NOT DISTURB

Fill 3½ in/9 cm pots with a loamless potting compost. Make a dibber hole in the centre and fill with sharpsand. Insert the prepared geranium cuttings into the sand plug for rooting. Your shoots will grow out from the sand core into the potting compost without having to be disturbed.

Ian Cooke
Head gardener, Ascott, Bucks

IN THE WINDOW

A jar of water on a sunny windowsill is all you need for propagating cuttings. Geraniums and carnations are easily rooted like this. Use the side shoots on the stems from a bunch of spray carnations to grow new plants.

Mrs Elizabeth Dorling
Springfield Cottage, Bucks

GAP FILLERS

I have a modest cold-frame in which I keep potted-up geraniums from previous seasons, fuchsia cuttings and cuttings of white *Campanula isophylla*. These are all brilliant for planting out to fill gaps in May or June and save quite a lot of money at garden centres. When taking geranium cuttings at the end of the year I find it useful to colour code them – and of course, white fits in everywhere.

Prunella Scales
Actress

SOWN IN THE POD

Lapageria rosea, the choice evergreen climber from Chile, is expensive to buy but easy to propagate from seed providing the following technique is used. Obtain a ripe seed pod and split it open. Leave the seeds in the pod and place each half flat on to seed compost, sprinkling more compost among the seeds. Most will germinate, whereas if sown dry away from the pod hardly any will.

John Humphris
Chairman, Professional Gardeners Guild

GROW A GIFT

Take cuttings of violas in the autumn from the centre of the plant. Place them deep into a mixture of half peat and half sharpsand, on top of 1½ in/3·8 cm of John Innes potting compost No. 2. They will root in the shade in five to six weeks. Give them away to friends in the spring, after potting them.

Richard G. M. Cawthorne
Viola and violetta specialist

DAISIES GALORE

It is easy to root cuttings of the marguerite *Argyranthemum frutescens foeniculaceum* in water if cut cleanly at a node, stripping the lower leaves. I have an old glass 'rose', a flower holder with many holes for stems. I stand this in about 1½ in/3·8 cm of water with a pinch of Phostrogen and insert a cutting in each hole. Those rooted in the autumn will have tips pinched out in the spring and potted on. The tips thus removed may

144

be rooted in the same way to make a second crop
of plants.

Nada Jennett
Horticultural lecturer and adviser

TAKING ROOT

When taking cuttings of daphnes, particularly
varieties like *Daphne odora*, which are often difficult
to get to root, try this method. Take the cuttings
when the plant is in full flower and put them in
water indoors, where all may enjoy the delicious
scent. When the flowers are over, allow the cuttings
to dry for twenty-four hours, then pot them up in
the usual way, keeping the atmosphere moist. A
surprising proportion will root and provide healthy
plants for setting out in a couple of years.

Dr C. R. Prior
Garden Master, Trinity College, Oxford

EARLY SHOOTS

Take young shoots from dahlias early in the season,
root and grow them on in small pots. The resulting
'pot tubers' are small and hard, and very easily
stored, ready to be planted out the following year.

Kenneth Vaughan
Gardener-in-Charge, Westbury Court Garden, Glos

PROPAGATING POPLAR

It's easy to propagate poplar trees. In the spring
break off a branch about 6 ft/1·8 m long and stick
the bottom 2 ft/0·6 m in the ground. Then all you
have to do is wait until next year when it will
have rooted. I had about 90 per cent success.

The late Rt Hon Lord Havers

145

RUNNING WILD

Silverweed, which is a very attractive ground cover in full sun or semi shade, is extremely easily propagated by runners. One plant will easily give you thirty additional plants.

Miriam Rothschild
Wild flower specialist

TWO-FORK TRICK

Hostas are improved by being split in the spring every three years or so. This is easily done if you dig the whole clump up and insert two forks, back to back, between the shoots. Push the handles apart and the roots will disentangle. Repeat as often as possible, replant the best bits and give the rest away.

Mrs John Falloon
Bowlands, New Zealand

THE WELL-EQUIPPED
GARDENER

MIND YOUR BACKS

Take great care in the early spring (even if it feels
quite warm) to put a warm scarf or sweater round
your middle when you do some digging in the
garden. An exposed back will lead to a very
painful one next morning.

Mrs B. S. Barlow
Stancombe Park, Glos

A WELL-DRESSED GARDENER

When I'm planting or weeding I like to kneel
down, so I wear skateboarders' knee-protectors and
I can crawl about in comfort. And I wear a light
nylon kagoul which has lots of pockets for secateurs, garden twine etc. It gives me great freedom
of movement, keeps out the cold and is easy to
wash and dry. If it starts to rain I just put up the
hood and carry on gardening.

Cynthia Ashford
Garden designer

147

DRIPS

I find thin cotton gloves worn under rubber ones quite the best sort of gardening glove. And for those who have a drip on the end of their noses when gardening in cold weather – what gardener doesn't? – a tennis sweat-band on the wrist over the rubber glove is a perfect wiper.

Mrs R. Goode
The Manor House, Bucks

FORMAL OCCASIONS

My grandmother left a drawerful of beautiful long above-the-elbow suede gloves. Now I wear them every summer when I'm cutting roses or picking gooseberries, and so avoid those disfiguring scratches these activities inevitably incur.

Mrs Camilla Strong

A DRY START

When you have finished gardening for the day, pin your gardening gloves together by the inside wrist-bands with a clothes peg and hang them over a nail in the wall. You will always have fresh, dry gloves next time you go to work in the garden.

Mrs Joy Pelham-Lane

FOOT-REST

An old gardener once told me that the best way to avoid tired feet is to put a geranium leaf under your heel, inside your sock. I've tried it and it seems to work.

Gerhard Bulle

DUTCH TREAT

Next time you're in Holland get some clogs. They are ideal gardening footwear: warm, mower-safe and waterproof, and they spread the weight when you're standing about on wet ground. On top of all that they are inexpensive and last for ever.

Jane Harris
Garden designer

HORRORS

Oh, the horror of a spider in your wellies! For peace of mind keep them out by covering the tops with stockings or cut-off legs of tights when you take the wellingtons off.

Charlotte Millar

SOAP STORY

Before you go gardening, save endless scrubbing after the work is done by putting soap under and round your nails.

Lady Maureen Fellowes

SOFT AND SWEET

Really grubby gardening hands can be soft as well as clean if you wash them in a mixture of sugar and washing-up liquid.

Mrs Kenneth Harper

MADE TO MEASURE

Measurements are often needed in the garden but a tape measure never seems to be to hand. It is a good idea to measure tools such as trowels and spade blades and make a mental note of the lengths to facilitate accurate spacing when planting. Most booted feet are, not surprisingly, about a foot long. An exact measurement of your boot length will help with quick spacing between rows and larger plants.

Ian Cooke
Head gardener, Ascott, Bucks

SEED DRILLS

Producing a uniform seed drill with a traditional draw hoe can be very difficult. Try using a triangular paint scraper which produces a much more even effect. Instead of a garden line, a straight-sided plank can be easier to use. On light sandy soils, drills can be prepared by lightly pressing a broom handle on to the soil.

Ian Cooke
Head gardener, Ascott, Bucks

EVER READY

Never go into the garden without a pair of secateurs.

The Lady Carrington
The Manor House, Bucks

THE CUTTING EDGE

One is always told of the importance of sharp secateurs and I keep a small steel file in my pocket so that I can sharpen the blades after almost every clipping.

Timothy Sergison Brooke
Chipping Warden Manor, Northants

GENTLE SQUEEZES

People who have a weak grip may like to know that there is a secateur which cuts through tough stems in stages. Instead of needing one big squeeze, this clipper has a ratchet action which allows up to four gentle squeezes to be made in order to complete the cut. It is called the CEKA Ratchet Pruner and is widely available from garden centres.

David Hollinrake
Horticultural therapist

A GOOD LITTLE TOOL

My wife is the grower and I am the destroyer. I clip and chop, prune and lift, mow and strim. I never go into the garden without two weapons in my pocket: a pair of secateurs and a folding pruning saw. The latter is a remarkable tool, light as a feather, folding neatly in the pocket with no nasty corners and yet extremely effective. With little effort it is possible to saw branches (and trees) up to 6 in/15 cm at least in diameter. It is, of course, made in Japan and called ARS. Advertised in The Royal Horticultural Society and Rose Society journals it is available by post from Burton McCall of Parker Drive, Leicester LEA OJP.

Commander L. M. M. Saunders Watson
Rockingham Castle, Leics

PONICA BUCKET

To keep spade, fork, hoe and similar tools clean and rust-proof with the minimum effort I use a 'ponica bucket'. In the garden where I spent my formative years there was a large bucket full of oil-impregnated sand kept conveniently close to the tool-shed door. Tools were rough cleaned after use, then plunged up and down in the sand to complete the burnishing process. The thin skin of oil left on the polished surface acted as a rust-proofing until the tools were needed again. Sump oil poured over builders' sand makes a cheap 'ponica bucket'.

Geoffrey Smith
Garden adviser and broadcaster

NO BENDING

As you know, all non-stainless-steel tools should be cleaned and oiled after use. When your lawn-mower has its sump renewed, drain the oil into a large tin. Buy a brush for painting old-fashioned radiators – like a large, very long-handled tooth-brush – and you will be able to oil your garden implements without bending and for nothing (except for the cost of the brush).

Charles Shepley-Cuthbert
Spring House, Northants

RUST PROOF

Garden tools, on coming into contact with earth or water, can easily become rusty if not thoroughly cleaned and dried. To avoid this, keep them in their original plastic wrappings, hang them in the shed and *never use them*. This will ensure years of rust-free use.

Victoria Wood

152

OFF TO A GOOD START

The start of a new gardening season is often heralded by a spring day and the sound of a lawn-mower purring across the grass – that is, as long as the mower will start. Caring for the engine will reduce this headache. At the end of the season, simply run the machine until it is out of fuel, clean the mower and blades, then store it in a dry place. Before starting the engine the following spring change the oil, clean the air filter and fill with newly bought petrol.

Tony Whitburn
Lawn-mower engine manufacturer

MAKE A DATE

Make a note in your diary on 29 December to book your motor mower in to be serviced, thereby ensuring early readiness for spring mowing.

Mrs S.Hoskins
Ashley Manor, Glos

STRING ALONG

Drill a hole in the lid of a large, screw-topped container and put a ball of string in it. Pull an end through the hole and the string will keep clean and dry and, above all, won't become tangled.

Albert Reed
Head gardener, Swyncombe House, Oxon

THE CUTTING EDGE

Before you use your cylinder mower in the spring, put a thin film of carburandum on the bottom blade to clean and bed in the cylinder.

Alan Philpott
Gardener, Upton House, Warw

SAFETY BELT

The only drawback to an electric mower or hedgecutter is the danger of cutting the wire. This can be avoided if you loop the wire through the belt of your trousers in front, over your shoulder and through your belt at the back. It will always stay behind you – especially if you start at the nearest point to the source of electricity and work away from it.

Gordon Welburn
Head gardener, Wardington Manor, Oxon

A CLEAN SWEEP

Sweeping leaves in the autumn is one of the most boring of recurring garden chores. Mowing them first makes it a lot easier. Set the blades of the mower high and drive over the leaves to chop them up. Most will be propelled into the lawn cuttings basket and the rest will just blow away.

Jeremy Saisse
Tractor manufacturer

NEW LABELS FOR OLD

Plastic labels which have been written on using a spirit-based 'permanent marker' can often be cleaned for re-use by rubbing them vigorously with a rag dampened with methylated or surgical spirit.

Bill Keen
Hon Editor, British Cactus and Succulent Journal

THE WINNER

We have a small London garden and one of our very best wedding presents was an automatic watering system.

Julian Fellowes

154

AN INVALUABLE GARDEN TOOL

Buy a second-hand garden fork with four prongs and take it to a blacksmith who will bend the tines under to make a 'claw'. This makes a wonderful implement for breaking up and aerating the soil around plants after trampling over the border when weeding, planting etc.

Annabel Allhusen
Garden designer

NO MORE BACKACHE

I am tall and long-handled edging shears are never long enough for me. Now, when I buy a new pair, I cut 10 in/25 cm off the old shears handles, take the handle-grips off the new pair and insert lengths of broom handle down the new shafts. When I have placed the old handle-grips over the top the shears are 10 in/25 cm longer and, hooray, no more backache.

M.Watkins
Gardener-in-Charge, Baddesley Clinton, Warks

CRACKED

One of the problems with paved areas in gardens is the weeds that grow between the stones. These are often very difficult to weedkill because of the proximity of cultivated plants. I find the best implement for removing these is a hoof-pick – at last a use for the 'thing to take stones out of horse's hooves'.

The Lord Porchester
Highclere, Berks

CUT TO THE QUICK

An old long-bladed knife with a serrated edge – such as a bread knife – is ideal for getting weeds out of cracks and crannies in paving. It is also the perfect tool for getting right to the bottom of a long-rooted weed such as a dandelion.

Vernon Russell-Smith
Garden designer

A CASE FOR SPLITTING

When hammering canes or stakes into the ground, put a spent cartridge case over the top to prevent splitting. A 28 bore does best for narrow canes and it can be used over and over again.

The Duke of Buccleuch
Boughton House, Northants

WOBBLE AID

If you are a bit unsteady on your feet, or use a walking stick or walking frame, transport your tools round the garden in a supermarket trolley. Ask the manager of your local supermarket for one or help the environment by removing one from the river.

Tim Spurgeon
Assistant director, Horticultural Therapy

SCOOP

A ½ gal/2 l plastic bottle, the sort with a handle, makes a wonderful scooper if it is cut diagonally from the cap down to the bottom corner nearest the handle. The wedge shape makes it ideal for cleaning gutters too.

The Viscountess Eccles

BIN IT

Digging or scooping silt out of a rubber-lined pond presents the hazard of puncturing or tearing the lining. The ideal tool for the job, which will do no damage at all, is a plastic dustbin.

Anthony Archer-Wills
Pond and water-garden specialist

SAFETY FIRST

Lock the tool shed. The value of the contents may be minimal but the easily accessible supply of spades, crowbars, ladders, garden trolleys and wheelbarrows could aid villains intent on removing garden statuary or gaining entry to the house.

Norman Hudson
Technical adviser, Historic Houses Association

BACK-TO-BACK

If, like me, you have a lean-to greenhouse back-to-back with a potting shed, install a small wood-burning stove in the latter and keep it going for six hours a day in winter. The greenhouse will stay frost-free provided it is lined with bubbly plastic and the door between it and the shed is kept open.

Sir Edward Tomkins
Winslow Hall, Bucks

ROLL OUT THE BARREL

When you've laddered a pair of tights or stockings, put the good foot over the down spout that fills your water barrel to filter out the dirt and leaves from the roof. And if you haven't got a water barrel, get one quickly. In times of falling water tables and drought no house should be without one.

Penelope Keith
Actress

WATER, WATER

In my opinion, one water butt is not enough. We have three placed next to one another, the first jacked up on a plinth two bricks high, the second a little lower and the third at ground level. A pipe from the top of one takes the water into the neighbouring butt, thus increasing one's water capacity threefold.

Mrs David White
Flint House, Bucks

SHADES

To shade the inside of your greenhouse in the summer, apply Summer Cloud or white emulsion paint with an old roller brush to the *inside* of the greenhouse. This is far safer than painting the outside by reaching over from steps or a ladder. In the autumn, hose the paint off on a damp, dewy morning when the condensation is high.

Walter Long
Professional gardener

SPARKLING GLASS

The outside of a greenhouse needs to be washed

every so often and this chore is easily and safely performed without a ladder if you use a long-handled squeegee mop.

Mrs Sandra Hendley

ABOUT THE HOUSE

CHRISTMAS ROSES

Almost the most precious of the winter flowers, *Helleborus niger*, the Christmas rose, is difficult to keep when cut. Now I find that if I prick the stems all the way from base to flower with a needle, place the flowers in a deep vase so that they are up to their necks in water, leave them for an hour or so and then place them in an ordinary vase as deep as is convenient, my Christmas roses will last for at least two or three days.

Hardy Amies
Fashion designer

WARM WATER TREATMENT

Having picked your *Helleborus orientalis*, the Lenten rose, put it *at once* in a vase of warm water covering at least three quarters of the stem. Leave for a few hours. Cut off the bottom ½ in/1·25 cm of the stem *under water* and transfer water and *Helleborus* to a permanent vase. With this treatment it will probably last for a week or longer.

Mary Readman
Garden designer

WHITE CURRANT

The pink flowers of flowering currant are welcome because they are among the first flowers of the spring, but I always think the colour of the common variety rather sickly. If you cut branches while they are still in bud and put them in water in a warm, dark place the flowers will be white when they come out.

The Hon. Lady Smith-Ryland
Sherbourne Park, Warks

PIN PRICKS

Wilting roses, perhaps ones that have had a long journey from the florist, can be revived by a long drink after crushing the end of the stem and then pushing a pin through just below the flower. This releases any air blocks and allows the water to get to the petals.

Mrs Nigel Azis
Chairman, National Gardens Scheme

BREAK THE BLOCKAGE

A tulip will last much longer in a vase if you prick the stem to its centre with a pin twice, about 1 in/2·5 cm below the flower and ½ in/1·25 cm below that. This breaks the vacuum and allows the flower to take up water.

Jan Leeming
Television presenter

MUD, GLORIOUS MUD

I have always liked Beverley Nichols' idea of half filling an opaque vase with earth, filling it to the brim with water, and then sticking a bunch of narcissus into the earth. The mud settles in half an hour and they look as if they are growing. They also last longer used in this way.

Elizabeth Jane Howard
Novelist

A SPOONFUL OF SUGAR

We add a lump of sugar to all our flower arrangements. There is no doubt in my mind that it makes them last longer. Occasionally I give them an aspirin as well.

The Duchess of Marlborough
Blenheim Palace, Oxon

FIZZY

Does everyone know that if you put lemonade instead of water into a vase of flowers, they will last twice as long? My husband says it works with fizzy water as well.

Eileen Atkins
Actress

ROADSIDIA

The 'secret' ingredient which top flower designers use in their arrangements is 'roadsidia': literally, material from the road side. Many of the world's best designers collect attractive weeds for filling out designs in unusual ways.

Tim Harrison
Editor, The Florist

EVER BEEN FOOLED?

You can make beautiful flower arrangements by using realistic silk flowers with fresh foliage. If you always use flowers that are in season or available at the florists, it is surprising how many people are not aware of the difference.

Mrs Elizabeth Dorling
Springfield Cottage, Bucks

FRAGRANCE

Pick viola blooms for that special dinner. They will soon scent the whole room with their fragrance.

Richard G. M. Cawthorne
Viola and violetta specialist

PUT IN THE PLUG

Few flowers are more glamorous than the tall spikes of delphiniums. We find that the best way to make them last a long time in water is to hold them upside down and fill the stem with water. Then insert a plug of cotton wool to keep the water in place.

The Duchess of Marlborough
Blenheim Palace, Oxon

LIFE IS CHEAP

To prolong the life of picked flowers, delphiniums in particular, place a twopenny piece at the bottom of the vase and then fill it with a mixture of water and lemonade.

The Lord Palumbo
Bagnor Manor, Berks

KINDEST CUT

When arranging gladiolus, nip out the top bud, and with any luck all the rest of the buds will open. And carnations should always be cut between the nodules – they drink better that way.

Eileen Warburton

OPTICAL ILLUSIONS

I use garden greenery to soften and 'stretch' expensive bought flowers.

Prue Leith
Cookery writer

HEADS UP

Gerberas are difficult flowers to keep looking good, as they will droop their heads. However, if they have a good soak in water which has a little bleach in it for about two hours before arranging, this problem should be solved.

Robert Hillier
Hilliers Garden Centres

LONGER LASTING

The flowers of woody-stemmed plants will last longer in a flower arrangement if they are soaked in about 4 in/10 cm of boiling water for roughly half an hour. Then fill the container to the top with fresh water and leave them overnight before arranging.

Mrs J. Nicholson
Bucksbridge House, Bucks

FLOOD WARNING

When using Oasis in any container, always leave a gap at the side to give room to replenish the water and so prevent a flood on a polished table or the church floor.

Eileen Warburton

TAPED

If you are arranging flowers in a glass vase, and you don't want to use Oasis, a few strips of narrow Sellotape across the top will keep the flowers in place.

The Lady Cowdray
Cowdray Park, Sussex

BOXED IN

I don't enjoy using Oasis, so I stuff my vases with sprigs of box. It doesn't make the water smell and is strong enough to hold even the longest-stemmed flowers in place.

Mrs Susan Paul
Maidwell Hall, Northants

LEAVES PRESERVED

If you are preserving beech leaves in glycerine solution (one part glycerine to two parts boiling water) first split the stems and put them in 2 in/ 6 cm of boiling water. This clears the stems of any airlock and enables the glycerine solution to be taken up more quickly.

Mrs Patricia Meadows
Flower arranger

SCENT UP

I sprinkle a few drops of pot-pourri oil on to a tissue to hide in an arrangement of dried flowers. This is an excellent way to freshen up your home.

Mrs D. G. Jones
Rose Cottage, Bucks

165

SHADES OF THE ORIENT

Deep crimson concentrated food dye is the secret to this innovative arrangement of sedums. Mix it with enough hot water in a vase to make a strong crimson solution; add some Chrystal to keep it fresh. Pick sedums in various stages of development, some almost green. Arrange them in the vase and if they begin to shrivel add more flowers and more tinted water. Eventually when all become dry allow the water to evaporate and fill any gaps with other dried material such as sprays of purple berberis preserved in coloured glycerine. The vase will glow with the colours of an oriental rug and last for many weeks. If it begins to look tired and dusty, a short spell in gentle rain will return it to its former glory.

Mrs Rupert de Zoete
Cecily Hill House, Glos

OPEN AND CLOSED

If dried helichrysum arrangements get dusty, spray them with water. They will close up and reopen later as good as new.

Mrs Francis Sitwell
Weston Hall, Northants

MOSSY MAGI

Use sphagnum moss to hide the wire or Oasis supporting a flower arrangement. I think this is particularly important with dried flowers.

Buzzy Lepper
'Fleurtation' Dried Flowers

BRIGHT AND BREEZY

Dried flowers will keep their colour if they are

kept out of bright sunlight and an occasional spray of water will stop them getting brittle.

Gill Harper
Dried flower specialist

GOLDEN WEDDING

Collect tins of spray paint in as many different shades of gold as you can find. Gather together as large a variety of dried flowers as you can muster. Fill a vase with Oasis and protect it with paper. Start arranging the flowers and as you go along, spray each flower lightly, one with one shade of paint, the next with another. The finished arrangement will be a picture in shimmering golds and will make an unusual, glorious and lasting golden wedding present.

Mrs Rupert de Zoete
Cecily Hill House, Glos

DON'T TURN ROUND

Always keep a Christmas cactus (*Schlumbergera* × *buckleyi*) facing the same way. If it gets turned round it will drop its flowers. I put a small mark on the front of the pot so that, if I move it, it will go back on the windowsill the same way round.

Frank Lovell

SPIDERS

Keep spider plants as dry as possible. They have fleshy, water-retentive roots and need almost nothing to drink. When they develop brown tips it is often due to over-watering.

Mrs Moran Caplat

167

SUMMER SOJOURN

Schlumbergera × buckleyi, the Christmas cactus and its near relative, *Rhipsalidopsis guartreri*, the Easter cactus, will enjoy a spell in the open air in the summer. Once all danger of frost is past, they can be hung (in their pots) from the branches of a tree and, apart from occasional watering if the weather is exceptionally dry, can be left to their own devices until early autumn. This treatment usually improves their flowering performance.

Bill Keen
Hon. Editor, British Cactus and Succulent Journal

ADDED COLOUR

In winter, mix a few artificial flowers in a pot or bowl of growing house plants.

The late Monica Dickens
Author

A NICE CUP OF TEA

Don't throw away old tea bags. Keep them in a big old jug, filled with cold water. The weak cold tea is a wonderful food for indoor plants – keeps them fresh and gives them a *very* long life. A once-a-week application is sufficient.

Mrs W. A. Palmer
Bussock Wood, Berks

PICK-ME-UP

If you have a sick-looking house plant that won't flower, give it two aspirins dissolved in 1 pt/600 ml lukewarm water. The salicylic acid in the aspirin comes closest to the natural growth hormone in plants and acts as a pick-me-up.

Nicholas Turrell
Horticulturist and journalist

WARM DOUCHE

Fill your watering-cans in the morning so that by evening they may be chambré and tender plants are not given a cold douche.

Mrs Heather Pegg

UNDER WATER

Indoor cyclamen will never fail if they are always watered from underneath.

Mrs Francis Sitwell
Weston Hall, Northants

ALE AND HEARTY

House plants much appreciate having their leaves wiped over with beer.

Josephine Ferrer

WHEN AND WHERE

Premature deaths in African violets can be avoided by watering *only* when the leaves wilt with drought. The plants will flower regularly if they are placed next to the glass in a north-facing window.

The Reverend Tony Clements
African Violet Centre, King's Lynn, Norfolk

BALANCED BOWLS

For people who like bowls of hyacinths indoors: plant bulbs individually in 3 in/7·5 cm pots, then when they are in flower, plant equal-sized ones into a large bowl so that you have flowers of the same height.

John Cordery
Head gardener, Paxmere House, Berks

LEVEL-HEADED

To help hyacinths planted in bowls to grow to a level height, fill the bowl with compost and then make a hole for each bulb, adding a sprinkling of silver sand before planting.

Walter Upton
Head gardener, Friars Well, Oxon

A SUCCESSION OF PAPER WHITES

Among the most satisfying of the winter indoor bulbs, with their heady scent and pristine flowers, Narcissus Paperwhite Grandiflora, will give you pleasure for weeks if you plant them in succession. Plant some in the normal way – in bowls which you leave outside until just before the frost – and put the rest in a polythene bag in the fridge. Take a few out each week or so and plant as before. It is worth remembering that they will flower six weeks after being planted.

The Hon. Mrs Sergison Brooke
Chipping Warden Manor, Northants

FRESH FINGERS

If you hate the smell of garlic on your fingers, grow it like chives on your kitchen windowsill. Peel five large cloves of garlic and plant them, leaving at least half the clove above the surface, in compost in a 5 in/12·5 cm terracotta pot. Keep them well watered and green shoots will appear. When they are tall enough, cut them and use them in your cooking pot.

Jan Leeming
Television presenter

YUMMY

If you like spaghetti, grow a pot of basil and keep it

on your kitchen shelf or windowsill, facing the sun. Wonderful with tomato sauce.

Rabbi Lionel Blue

DON'T TURN ROUND

As a flower spike develops on an orchid, try not to alter its position in relation to the light source, as moving can result in a twisted or curved flower spike.

Lucinda Lachelin
Orchid grower, Royal Horticultural Society Gardens,
Wisley

FLOWER POWER

Phalaenopsis, or moth orchids, make successful house plants in today's centrally heated houses. One way of getting maximum flower production is to cut back the flower spikes just as the last flowers on them are beginning to fade. If they are removed to a joint about 3–4 in/7·5–10 cm above where they arise, a new branch should be formed, which in good conditions should bear a new flush of flowers in around three months' time.

Christopher Bailes
Curator, Royal Horticultural Society Gardens, Wisley

FAIL SAFE

Cymbidiums – no fail. September to May, keep on a light windowsill free from frost, put under a running tap for ten minutes once a fortnight. Summer in the garden, pour through 2 gal/9 l of feed every two weeks. They like being pot-bound.

The Hon. Mrs Tyser

FINGER TEST

Orchids suffer if they are over-watered. Half a teacup a week is usually sufficient and if, when you push two joints of your little finger into the pot you feel any moisture there, don't water at all.

Bill Gaskell
Orchid grower, Woodstock Orchids

NEAT AND TIDY

Splitting the dead leaves of cymbidiums along the mid-rib makes it easy to pull the two halves away tidily. Remove too those old leaf bases from around the pseudobulbs, where pests and diseases can lurk. It makes the plant neater, too.

Lucinda Lachelin
Orchid grower, Royal Horticultural Society Gardens, Wisley

STRONG AND GENTLE

I find nylon fishing line useful for tying some species of orchid to cork rafts or old branches. It is transparent, long-lasting and gentle with the plant.

Lucinda Lachelin
Orchid grower, Royal Horticultural Society Gardens, Wisley

GOLDEN CHAINS

For an exotic indoor tree take a tip from Beverley Nichols: grow a young laburnum in your green-house or conservatory where it will produce its perfect golden chains well before its outdoor brethren.

Miranda Innes
Garden editor, Country Living

SHOWING OFF

To show a potted climber to advantage, so that its flowers are well displayed and it is well ventilated, don't grow it over the traditional pyramid of canes, which tend to bunch it at the top. Instead, insert four tall canes at the sides of the pot and push a nice rounded hoop of wire into the top of each opposite cane and tie the hoops together where they cross. I grow lapagerias, hoyas etc. this way.

Orlando Murrin
Deputy editor, Living

SELF-SUFFICIENT

I am setting up an indoor water garden which, at the moment of writing, contains nothing but water, gravel and two pieces of extremely special wood – a sort of Japanese effect. This will eventually be planted for me by a keen young expert from Hambridge Fisheries outside Taunton – a wonderland for any fish or pond lover – and, unlike dying unwatered cyclamen and wilting vases of roses, it will look after itself and greet me with flourishing foliage, even after a three-week absence. Or that is my hope. The expert tells me that I might even be allowed in good time two small self-sufficient indoor fish that will never need feeding. A delightful prospect.

Margaret Drabble
Author

THIS AND THAT

THE PERFECT PRESENT

I like to give my friends and family plants for the garden. However I have learnt that it is better to fly in the face of correctitude in these matters and demand of the recipient exactly what would suit. So many different factors from soil to scent can turn a well-meant offering into an unsuitable dud. A good point about giving plants or trees as a commemorative gift is that if by chance they fail to grow, they can be replaced by the beneficiary, and the original thought is conserved.

Drusilla Beyfus
Writer, editor and broadcaster

FOILED

If you possess a garden which is some way from inhabited buildings and accessible from a public highway make sure that you have a *very secret* nursery tucked away somewhere. Thieves of good small shrubs abound, alas. If practicable (as with, for instance, rhododendrons) don't plant out shrubs small enough to tempt robbers. One must wait until they are at least 2 ft/0·6 m high and preferably bushy.

The Marquess of Anglesey
Plas-Newydd, Anglesey

BLUEBELL GLUE

The sap from bluebell stalks makes an excellent adhesive. According to William Turner in his *Herbal* of 1568: 'The boyes of Northumberland scrape the roote of the herbe and glew theyr awn arrowes and bokes wyth that slyme that they scrape of.' Geoffrey Grigson decided to test this, and glued the endpapers of his notebook. Thirteen years later it was still intact.

Elizabeth Jane Howard
Novelist

REFRESHERS

Whenever you undertake a long car journey, pick a stem of angelica leaves and put it under the passenger's feet with instructions to tread on it every half hour or so. The effect is to refresh the driver and the air in the car, exercise the passenger and help prevent travel sickness. Armfuls of mint or lemon verbena can likewise be used.

Lesley Bremness
Herb grower and garden designer

POLLEN COUNT

If you get lily pollen on your clothes, curtains or lampshades use a bit of Sellotape to get it off; never use water or rub it as it will then stain for ever.

Mrs Michael Todhunter
The Old Rectory, Berks

BURN BALM

Worried about the ozone layer and possible sun-burning? Nature's answer is the aloe, which grows vigorously indoors or in a heated greenhouse. The sticky sap from a fleshy leaf can give vital protection to the gardener's face and forearms, plus considerable and immediate relief to the accident-prone cook. A staple ingredient in many expensive sunburn remedies, the aloe is not only extremely easy to grow and divide – it's also free!

Michael O'Halloran
Littleworth Farm, Bucks

TASTY TREATS

Pastry offcuts can be pressed round the knotted end of a piece of string about 1 ft/0·3 m long, in a rough bell shape. Bake at the same time as a tart and hang them outside the kitchen window for the birds. For a Christmas or Easter treat, press Trill birdseed into the pastry before baking.

Orlando Murrin
Deputy editor, Living

BIRD MUGS

Whenever I have bacon fat – or any fat – over, I put it in an old mug and mix in some birdseed. I then hang the mug on a line and watch the birds feast to their hearts' delight.

Lady Sophia Schilitzi
The Old Vicarage, Northants

NESTING POTS

To make a long-lasting and inexpensive haven for small birds, take a clay flowerpot 8–10 in/20–25 cm in diameter and chip open the bottom hole to

176

at least 1½ in/3·8 cm so that small birds can get in. Put a little moss or nesting material in the pot and fasten it, very firmly, so that the top is against a wall or flat surface of a tree – perhaps where a branch has been sawn off – using copper or aluminium wire and at least three galvanized nails. Put it high where small boys can't reach it, and enjoy watching the birds.

The Lord Ridley
Blagdon, Northum

MRS TIGGYWINKLE

Hedgehogs are good in the garden because they eat slugs. But never give them saucers of milk. This gives them diarrhoea and they die. If you must put food out for them, give them a raw egg and a supply of clean drinking water.

Mrs Roy Petrie

SHUN THE SUN

When you visit a garden on a cloudy day, don't leave your camera at home. Bright sun, just the thing for long views, will ruin any attempt at close-ups. For the best plant portraits, dull and cloudy skies, and a steady hand, will provide the best results.

Hugh Palmer
Garden photographer

LEARN ABOUT FLOWERS

Try drawing a flower in all its bits. You will then probably remember what it looks like and its name for all time.

Richard Nutt
Great Barfield, Bucks

GET DOWN TO IT

Since gardens are mostly green with colourful bits, a photograph of a large area can be disappointingly colourless. Don't attempt to photograph the whole but concentrate on a small area of colour and get in amongst it and *down* to it. The only time you should take a general view is of a knot garden taken from an upstairs window.

Jeremy Whitaker
Architectural and horticultural photographer

MEMORIES THAT NEVER FADE

To get the best out of visiting gardens open to the public, go late in the afternoon when the light is softer than in the middle of the day (specially important if you take photographs). Go round once just enjoying the garden and getting the feel of it, then with a notebook writing down the plant names, plant associations and design ideas that appeal to you. Make sketches, too. Without a written record, garden memories often fade into a jumble of pretty scenes.

Anne Scott-James
Journalist

FORGET IT NOT

When visiting a friend's garden, take a notebook and write down the name of the garden as well as the plants you wish to remember – it is surprising how easy it is to forget where you saw what.

The Lady Carrington
The Manor House, Bucks

BEST SEEN

Keen visitors to other people's gardens will want to

choose the best from the thousands available. I believe that there are about one hundred 'top' gardens in Britain and Ireland of which most are National Trust or stately homes. Of the number of private gardens I particularly recommend three: 23 Beechcroft Road, Oxford; Newcastle House, West Road, Bridgend, Mid Glamorgan, Wales; and Folly Farm, Sulhamstead, Reading, Berkshire. In Scotland, don't miss Little Sparta, Lanarkshire.

Peter King
Editor, Good Gardens Guide

INDEX OF HINTS

INDEX OF NAMES